Focus on Content-Based Language Teaching

Oxford Key Concepts for the Language Classroom series

Focus on Assessment
Eunice Eunhee Jang

Focus on Content-Based Language Teaching
Patsy M. Lightbown

Focus on Oral Interaction
Rhonda Oliver and Jenefer Philp

Focus on Content-Based Language Teaching

Patsy M. Lightbown

Great Clarendon Street, Oxford, OX2 6DP, United Kingdom

Oxford University Press is a department of the University of Oxford.
It furthers the University's objective of excellence in research, scholarship, and education by publishing worldwide. Oxford is a registered trade mark of Oxford University Press in the UK and in certain other countries

First published in 2014
2018 2017 2016 2015 2014
10 9 8 7 6 5 4 3 2 1

ISBN: 978 0 19 400082 6

Printed in China

This book is printed on paper from certified and well-managed sources

ACKNOWLEDGEMENTS

The authors and publisher are grateful to those who have given permission to reproduce the following extracts and adaptations of copyright material: p139 Figure from Cummins, J. (2000). *Language, power and pedagogy: Bilingual and children in the crossfire*. Clevedon, England: Multilingual Matters. Reproduced by permission. p75, 83 Extract from 'The helping behaviours of fifth graders while using collaborative strategic reading during ESL content classes' by J. Klingner and S. Vaughn, TESOL Quarterly 34/ Wiley-Blackwell. Reproduced by permission. p69 Extract from 'Content-based language teaching in China: contextual influences on implementation' by Philip Hoare, *Journal of Multilingual & Multicultural Development*, 1 Feb 2010 Taylor & Francis, reprinted by permission of the publisher (Taylor & Francis Ltd, http://www.tandf.co.uk/journals). p6 Table from 'Time on task and immersion graduates' French proficiency' by Turnbull, M., Lapkin, S., Hart, D., & Swain, M. in *French second language education in Canada: Empirical studies* (pp. 31–55). Toronto: University of Toronto Press. Reproduced by kind permission of Dr Miles Turnbull and Dr Sharon Lapkin. p307 Extract from 'Cognitive content engagement in content-based language teaching' by Stella Kong and Philip Hoare, *Focus on Content Based Languages Teaching*, Volume 15 Issue 3, p320, copyright © 2011 by SAGE. Reprinted by Permission of SAGE. p124 Extract from within Catherine Doughty, Jessica Williams (eds) *Focus on Form in Classroom Second Language Acquisition*, 1998. © Cambridge University Press, reproduced with permission.

To my children and grandchildren.
And to their father and grandfather.

Contents

Acknowledgments

In writing this book, I have benefited from the experience and insights of educators and researchers who have sought to understand and to improve students' opportunities to learn language and to learn academic content taught in a new language. Many of their names appear in the text and in the reference list, but it was not possible to include all of the important and valuable publications I have learned from. I only hope that I have acknowledged all of those whose work I have drawn on directly. I am grateful to the teachers and teacher educators whose classes and workshops have shaped my understanding of CBLT. Special thanks to the staff and students in the dual immersion program at the Christopher Columbus Family Academy, where I have seen wonderful examples of CBLT in action.

I am grateful to Oxford University Press, especially to Julia Bell and Ann Hunter for their support and attention to detail. Several colleagues have helped me identify and locate valuable materials among the thousands of publications relevant to CBLT. I thank Roy Lyster and Howard Nicholas for their help. Finally, my friend, colleague, and frequent co-author Nina Spada has been an important part of this project since we began working together on this *Key Concepts for the Language Classroom* series. She is a constant source of encouragement, reality checks, and laughter. I cannot thank her enough.

Series Editors' Preface

The Oxford Key Concepts for the Classroom series is designed to provide accessible information about research on topics that are important to second language teachers. Each volume focuses on a particular area of second/foreign-language learning and teaching, covering both background research and classroom-based studies. The emphasis is on how knowing about this research can guide teachers in their instructional planning, pedagogical activities, and assessment of learners' progress.

The idea for the series was inspired by the book *How Languages are Learned*. Many colleagues have told us that they appreciate the way that book can be used either as part of a university teacher education program or in a professional development course for experienced teachers. They have commented on the value of publications that show teachers and future teachers how knowing about research on language learning and teaching can help them think about their own teaching principles and practices.

This series is oriented to the educational needs and abilities of school-aged children (5–18 years old) with distinct chapters focusing on research that is specific to primary- and secondary-level learners. The volumes are written for second language teachers, whether their students are minority-language speakers learning the majority language or students learning a foreign language in a classroom far from the communities where the language is spoken. Some of the volumes will be useful to 'mainstream' teachers who have second language learners among their students, but have limited training in second/foreign language teaching. Some of the volumes will also be primarily for teachers of English, whereas others will be of interest to teachers of other languages as well.

The series includes volumes on topics that are key for second language teachers of school-age children and each volume is written by authors whose research and teaching experience have focused on learners and teachers in this age group. While much has been written about some of these topics, most publications are either 'how to' methodology texts with no explicit link to research, or academic works that are designed for researchers and post-graduate students who require a thorough scholarly treatment of the research, rather than an overview and interpretation for classroom practice. Instructors in programs for teachers often find that the methodology texts lack the academic background appropriate for a university course and that the scholarly works are too long, too difficult, or not sufficiently classroom-oriented for the needs of teachers and future teachers. The volumes in this series are intended to bridge that gap.

The books are enriched by the inclusion of *Spotlight Studies* that represent important research and *Classroom Snapshots* that provide concrete examples of teaching/learning events in the second language classroom. In addition, through a variety of activities, readers will be able to integrate this information with their own experiences of learning and teaching.

We are pleased to launch the series with this volume *Focus on Content-Based Language Teaching.*

Introduction

In schools all over the world, students are taught their academic subjects—mathematics, science, history—in a language that is not the one they learned at home. They are challenged to understand difficult new ideas, ask and answer questions, present reports, and sometimes take examinations in a language they are still learning. More and more teachers find that they need to be prepared to work with language learners in their classes.

Educational approaches that combine instruction in a new language and academic subjects are referred to as content-based language teaching (CBLT). CBLT is a major part of the education of millions of children, and that number is growing. For children who are immigrants or members of a minority-language group, going to school means learning a new language. For members of majority-language groups, proficiency in another language is seen as a way to enhance personal and professional opportunities. For both these groups, CBLT combines language learning with ongoing academic work.

The purpose of this book is to explore the possibilities and challenges of CBLT in primary and secondary schools in a variety of settings. The book will be of interest to educators who are new to this approach and to experienced CBLT teachers who want to add to their professional knowledge about the origins, achievements, and continuing evolution of this way of teaching.

Chapter 1 provides descriptions of some of the many different ways that CBLT has been implemented for students who have a variety of options and goals in learning a new language.

In Chapter 2 we will look at some findings and implications of research in education, psychology, and language acquisition that help to explain the principles underlying CBLT.

In Chapters 3 and 4, the focus will be on research that has been carried out in CBLT classrooms. In Chapter 3, we will review studies done with young learners—from pre-kindergarten through about age 11. In Chapter 4, research with 12- to 18-year old learners will be reviewed. In these chapters, we will examine research in both foreign-language and second-language (L2) settings, in schools where students receive all of their instruction in the new language and others where some academic subjects are taught in the students' first language (L1). The emphasis will be on relationships between what happens in classrooms and students' learning outcomes, in terms of both academic content knowledge and second language development.

Chapter 5 will provide a summary of the most important points covered in detail in the earlier chapters.

Some of the studies we review will be designated as Spotlight Studies. These are important not only because of what the researchers discovered, but also because the studies exemplify the different approaches that are used to look for answers to questions about how educational programs can most effectively help students learn both academic content and a new language at the same time. Each chapter will include Classroom Snapshots—brief descriptions or transcriptions of interaction between teachers and students or between students and their peers in CBLT classes. Naturally, brief snapshots cannot capture a whole program of instruction or even a single lesson. Nevertheless, they provide concrete examples of how teachers and learners cope with the opportunities and challenges of CBLT and allow us to connect our discussion of general principles to moments in real classrooms. In addition, each chapter will include some Activities that invite you to deepen your understanding of underlying questions, assumptions, or research findings through personal reflection, interacting with language learners and teachers, or doing some research of your own.

An annotated list of Suggestions for Further Reading will highlight some of the many excellent sources that have been consulted in the writing of this book. The Glossary provides definitions of terms that may either be unfamiliar to some readers or have a special meaning in the context of CBLT. These terms will be in bold print the first time they appear in the text, and the Index will allow you to find other mentions of them. The References section will provide complete information for all the sources that are cited in the chapters.

It is no exaggeration to say that there are thousands of articles, reports, and books on CBLT. A new journal devoted exclusively to research in this area has just been launched. This book is intended to introduce some of the findings and recommendations that have arisen from the research and from the experience of teachers and students over the years.

1 Approaches to CBLT

Preview

Content-based language teaching (CBLT) is an approach to instruction in which students are taught **academic content** in a language they are still learning. CBLT is inherent in **second language** contexts, where immigrant or **minority-language** students must learn both a new language and academic subjects at the same time. In foreign-language settings, CBLT may be introduced as an enrichment program to give **majority-language** students more time and more varied opportunities for using the language. In this chapter, we will see how CBLT has been implemented in a variety of school settings.

Read Classroom Snapshots 1.1 and 1.2. Think about similarities and differences in the interaction between the teachers and the students. What is the topic of the discussion? Who talks? Who listens? Who learns something new? What do they learn? How is language learned or practiced?

Classroom Snapshot 1.1

An English lesson in a Grade 3 classroom in the USA: Nearly all the students come from Hispanic backgrounds. Some speak mostly English at home; others speak Spanish as their home language. All students have had about half their schooling in English and half in Spanish since kindergarten. Teacher A sees the students for about 30 minutes a week, for a lesson that is focused on reading and writing English.

Teacher A: I want you to tell me about your spring break. Tell me in a complete sentence what you did on your spring break. First, I'll tell you what I did. On my spring break, I visited my sister in California.

Student 1: On my spring break, I went to New York.

Teacher A: Did you go with your parents?

Student 1: No, with my grandma.

Student 2: On my spring break, I went to the park.

Teacher A: The weather was great, wasn't it? Did you ride your bike?

Student 2: Yes.
Student 3: On my spring break, I played with my friends.
Teacher A: Nice.
Student 4: On my spring break, I went to the hospital to see my aunt.
Teacher A: Was she sick?
Student 4: She was in an accident.
Teacher A: Is she all right?
Student 4: Yes, she went home now.
Teacher A: Good.
Student 5: On my spring break, I have a sleepover with my friends.
Teacher A: You had a sleepover? At your house?
Student 5: Yes.
Teacher A: Who did something really exciting?
Student 6: I go to Disneyworld.
Teacher A: On my spring break, I …
Student 6: I went to Disneyworld.
Teacher A: That is exciting.

Classroom Snapshot 1.2

A mathematics lesson with the same Grade 3 students: Teacher B is with the students for most of every school day in alternate weeks, teaching all subjects in Spanish. Another teacher is with the students every other week, teaching all subjects in English. The lesson in Classroom Snapshot 1.2 was taught in Spanish and is translated here.

Teacher B does a brief review of multiplication. Students quickly and accurately provide the answers as she writes examples such as 3 × 2 and 4 × 2 on the board. Then she writes 3 × 4 × 2 on the board.

Teacher B: Who knows how to do this one? Can we multiply three numbers?
Several students: You can't do that.
Teacher B: Why not?
Sandra: You have to multiply two numbers.
Teacher B: Are you sure? Who thinks you can do this? Hector, do you want to try?
Hector: [comes to the board and writes 3 × 4 = 12 and 4 × 2 = 8]
Teacher B: What do you think, class? Is that how you do it? Who has another idea? Natalie.
Natalie: [comes to the board and writes 3 × 4 = 12 and then stops]
Teacher B: What do you think she should do next?
Students: Multiply by 2.

Teacher B: Multiply what by 2?
Students: 12.
Teacher B: [writes 12 × 2 = ...] What is 12 times 2?
Students: 24.
Teacher B: Is this the answer? Thumbs up if you agree. [Half the students raise their thumbs.] Thumbs down if you don't agree. [A few students show disagreement.] Show me [by a hand wobble] if you don't know. [A few students show uncertainty.]

(After two more examples, there is agreement—by a show of thumbs—that you multiply the first two numbers and then multiply the product of those numbers by the third number.)

Teacher B: So, who can tell me how to multiply three numbers?
Richard: Multiply the first two numbers. [Several seconds elapse; teacher waits.]
Teacher B: What's next, Richard?
Richard: Multiply the last number.
Teacher B: Multiply what?
Richard: Multiply the first numbers and then the last number.
Teacher B: Yes, I think you know how to do it. Can someone else explain how we do this?
Tomás: Multiply the first two numbers, then multiply the product by the last number.
Teacher B: Yes, and I like the way Tomás used the technical word 'product'. Now, is there another way we can do this?

Note: Unpublished data based on field notes from classroom observations by the author. Some details are adapted to preserve anonymity or to simplify the presentation. ■

Some readers may think that Classroom Snapshots 1.1 and 1.2 are shown for the purpose of contrasting approaches to teaching that are 'good' or 'not so good.' That is not the intention. Interestingly, readers might disagree about which is which! The most important thing to say about these two snapshots is that, depending on the other things that happen in this classroom and in the children's overall learning environment, both kinds of interaction can contribute to their learning. Each teacher has a different focus: one is focused primarily on teaching *language*; the other is focused primarily on teaching *content*.

In Classroom Snapshot 1.1, the teacher's goal is to practice language patterns that the students are familiar with and that they can produce with relative ease. Such practice can help students develop **fluency** in their use of these patterns. Furthermore, in this case, the teacher is also preparing the students to focus on a new pattern that is less familiar and requires more concentration. In the next activity, the students will write a little piece about 'something different' they 'would like to do' for their next vacation. Notice that even though the teacher is focused on a quick round of fluency practice, he still listens to each student and responds to what the student says as well as to how it is said.

In Classroom Snapshot 1.2, the teacher's focus is on making sure that students understand a new mathematical operation. She does more of the talking than the students, but she gives them plenty of time to answer when she asks a question. She listens to their answers and builds on what they can say. She encourages the use of mathematical language, but pays attention primarily to whether students know how to multiply three numbers.

We will return to these classroom examples and see many others as we explore the complex realities of content-based language teaching.

What is Content-Based Language Teaching?

What sets CBLT apart from other kinds of instruction is the expectation that students can learn—and teachers can teach—both academic subject matter content and a new language at the same time. With adequate preparation and resources, this expectation has been fulfilled in a number of different educational environments. In other situations, however, students have failed to reach the desired levels of either language proficiency or subject matter knowledge.

Educational outcomes are affected by many things. Some of these, such as population movement, poverty, parents' education, and legislation, are largely beyond the control of teachers and students and outside the scope of this book. While some of these factors will be mentioned as we seek to understand CBLT in different contexts, our focus will be on the interaction of teachers and learners within the CBLT classroom. One of the goals of this book is to identify the elements of CBLT that are associated with students' success in learning *both* a new language *and* academic content.

What do you think about content-based language teaching? Before we begin our exploration of research and practice, take a few minutes to reflect on how you think CBLT works for teachers and students.

Activity 1.1

The statements below represent views that some people hold about CBLT. Read each statement and check one of the columns to indicate how much you agree or disagree with it.

SA = Strongly Agree *A = Agree* *D = Disagree* *SD = Strongly Disagree*

	SA	A	D	SD
1 In CBLT, if students understand the academic content, language learning will take care of itself.				
2 It is not appropriate for teachers to correct students' language errors during content-based lessons.				
3 Second language learners in CBLT should use the same instructional materials as students who are already proficient in the language of instruction.				
4 It is best to begin CBLT after students have developed good reading skills in their L1.				
5 Students in CBLT need to have grammar and vocabulary instruction that is separate from content-based lessons.				
6 Teachers often fail to distinguish between a student's language abilities and subject matter knowledge.				
7 Students with learning or speech and language disabilities will have more difficulty in CBLT than they would in L1 instruction.				
8 CBLT is effective mainly because it allows students to spend more time using their L2.				
9 In CBLT, teachers should sometimes use the students' L1.				
10 In CBLT, students should be discouraged from using their L1.				
11 Cooperative learning and other types of group-work are not appropriate for CBLT, especially if students have the same L1.				
12 It is important to explicitly teach students the special language features that are typical of different academic subject matter.				
13 CBLT works when students' L1 is a language that is similar to the language of instruction (for example, English and French) but not when the languages are very different (for example, Chinese and English).				
14 Only native speakers of the language of instruction can be successful CBLT teachers.				

Once you have reflected on what *you* think about these statements, ask others what their reactions are. For example, ask a teacher who works with second language learners; ask an adult who learned his or her second language at school; ask a young person who is learning a second language at school. Do they agree? What are the points of greatest disagreement? What do you think the reasons might be for these differences? Discuss your findings with those of your classmates. Summarize your findings, paying special attention to any that surprise you. Refer to your notes from time to time as you read the remaining pages of this book. Be on the lookout for new information that may support your current views or raise questions about them. We will return to these statements in Chapter 5.

Where Do We Get Our Ideas about Teaching and Learning?

It has been observed that, although most people would be reluctant to tell a doctor how to treat a disease or a mechanic how to repair a car, many people are pretty sure they know how teachers ought to teach. No doubt this is due in part to the fact that we have all had many hours of experience as students in a classroom. Lortie (1975) referred to this as the 'apprenticeship of observation' and this apprenticeship forms the basis for many of our beliefs about what effective teaching is. The way we were taught affects the way we teach. We remember teachers we liked or didn't like, those from whom we felt we learned a great deal, and those who disappointed us. We may remember specific types of learning activities that we enjoyed and others that seemed pointless. We may, as it is often suggested, teach as we were taught, or we may try hard to make sure we do not repeat those aspects of our educational experience that we did not like.

Our experiences as learners also influence our specific expectations for learning a second language at school. Some students spend years in foreign language classes but never learn to use the language outside class; others find that the classroom learning prepares them well for continuing to learn the language when they travel to a place where they need to use it in daily life. Many people have had the experience of arriving at school as immigrant children with no knowledge of the language of instruction and going on to excel in both the new language and the academic subject matter. For others, the experience of being an immigrant or minority-language child at school was so frustrating that they left school before achieving success in either language or education.

We cannot escape the fact that our own experiences and those of people we know affect our views about what it takes to learn a new language and to succeed at school. However, as any parent of more than one child and any teacher of more than one class knows, there is a vast amount of individual variation in the way people learn and in what motivates them to keep at it when it gets difficult. Furthermore, there are great differences in the way an individual's learning preferences and abilities interact with the instructional environment, including the dynamics of a student's peer group, the attitudes and expectations of the larger society, and the facilities and tools available to promote learning.

Personal experiences and expectations are an essential element in our preparation for teaching. However, because of the differences among individual learners and their circumstances, it is also important to examine our instructional practices in light of what other students, educators, and researchers have learned in a variety of language learning and teaching conditions. In addition, when we measure the success of teaching, we need to think of learning outcomes not just in terms of students' test scores but also in terms of their identity and self-esteem and their attitudes toward education.

If we draw conclusions only from personal anecdotes or the experience of only one type of learner or one teaching situation, or if we use only one measure of learning outcomes, we may fail to take advantage of approaches and techniques that have proven effective for many learners. By informing ourselves about the findings of research, both **qualitative** and **quantitative**, and the experience of learners and teachers in a number of different situations, we can avoid drawing premature conclusions about how to provide effective instruction and what to expect from learners.

In reading this book, you will become familiar with the ways in which CBLT has been implemented and assessed by educators and researchers around the world. We will seek to understand the successes and limitations of this approach to learning a new language. We will ask how students can master academic content that is taught through a language they are still learning. We will also ask whether successful content learning ensures successful language learning. We will explore ways in which understanding the challenges of learning both content and language can inform and enlighten us as we work in settings where CBLT is already in place or as we consult with colleagues and parents who are considering its implementation.

The two Classroom Snapshots in the opening pages of this chapter exemplify the contrast between a lesson where English is the focus of teaching and learning and one where the primary focus is on the academic content. Look again at those snapshots. Pay special attention to the teacher's response to what students say in each snapshot. What do you think students will notice in the teacher's response? What do you think the teacher would like them to notice ... and remember?

Is CBLT More Effective than Traditional Language Instruction?

There are several assumptions about why CBLT might be preferred over instruction in which the second or foreign language is taught as one subject, separate from other academic content.

CBLT can be *efficient*. Students learn science, history, mathematics, or other subjects in lessons that are taught in a language they are still learning. In foreign language settings, this 'two for one' approach can increase the amount of time students spend in contact with the new language without taking time away from their regular curriculum. In second language settings, students can continue to make progress in their academic subjects while they are still learning the new language.

CBLT can be *motivating*. Because the academic content must be learned, students are more motivated to learn the new language than they might be in classroom activities designed to teach the language only. Engaging students in meaningful interaction that challenges them in cognitively age-appropriate ways can help to maintain their interest while their language skills grow. The consequences of not understanding the academic content are substantial and real as students prepare for examinations and further study.

CBLT can promote *advanced proficiency*. Learning subject matter content entails the use of academic styles of grammar and discourse as well as increasingly varied and sophisticated vocabulary. This prepares students for further academic, personal, or work-related language use outside the classroom.

We will see that these assumptions have been supported by research in CBLT classes at the primary and secondary level. We will also see that to reach age-appropriate levels of ability in the new language and to learn challenging academic content, students need time and the guidance of well-prepared teachers.

How is CBLT Implemented?

In preparation for reading about research that has been done in various CBLT environments, let us review some of the models for teaching academic content to students through the medium of a second or foreign language. This approach to education is implemented throughout the world, and although these classes share the basic goals of ensuring that students develop knowledge of both a new language and the academic content, the expectations for achievement range widely.

In a foreign-language context, the focus of CBLT instruction will typically be on improving the language skills of learners who have little contact with the language outside school. The expectation is that CBLT will give students greater access to the new language, in terms of both the amount of time they spend using the language and the quality and variety of language they will encounter. In some settings, the instruction may emphasize students' ability to read and understand academic material rather than the acquisition of oral language **proficiency**. Unless learners have friends or family members who speak the language or have opportunities to use the language in a full range of social, personal, and workplace environments, they will not achieve the kind of proficiency that makes them sound like **native speakers**. Nevertheless, their achievement of good comprehension skills and the ability to use the language for travel or study abroad and for cultural enrichment are considered evidence that the instructional program is a success.

In a second-language context, when CBLT is implemented in classrooms where immigrants or members of minority-language groups are learning the majority or official language, the expectations are likely to be considerably higher. Students are expected to learn the subject matter, to be sure, and they are also expected to achieve a level of language proficiency that will eventually allow them to continue their studies and professional training in the new language. That is, they are expected to have language skills that are comparable to those of native speakers who have learned this language from earliest childhood. If they do not reach these high levels of proficiency, there will be questions about the success of their educational experience.

Such differences in learning situations and in expectations sometimes lead to confusion about what can be accomplished through second language instruction in general and through CBLT in particular. For this reason, it is essential to look at CBLT, and indeed at any educational program, in its own setting and to avoid assumptions based only on comparisons of test scores or on anecdotal reports or even summaries of research findings that attempt to generalize from one context to another.

Let's begin by looking at some of the most familiar examples of CBLT around the world. First, a note on terminology: 'L1' will be used to refer to the language or languages that learners first acquired at home; 'L2' refers to the language or languages that they learn subsequently. In some cases, L2 may actually be a third or fourth additional language. As suggested above, it will sometimes be useful to distinguish between foreign-language and second-language settings. The former refers to settings where students do not typically hear the new language outside the classroom in which they are studying. The term 'second language' refers to a language being learned in a context where it is also used in the local community and where it is assumed that students will need to use that language in their daily lives, for further education and for employment. This distinction can lead to some odd sorts of labels. For example, French could be seen as a foreign language in some parts of Belgium, Canada, or Switzerland. In all three countries, French is an official language but there are regions where it is not typically used outside the language classroom. In some minority-language communities, residential patterns and socioeconomic divisions may isolate students from speakers of the majority language. The terminology is meant to characterize the language learning opportunities rather than the legal status of different languages.

CBLT for Majority-Language Students

The term 'majority-language students' is used here to refer to students whose L1 is the language that is most widely spoken in their immediate community or one that is considered to have equal status with other community languages. CBLT for majority-language students is a *choice*—made by parents, students, or school systems—that is intended to enhance the educational opportunities of students who already enjoy the benefits of belonging to a language group with high socioeconomic and/or political status. For example, the benefits of knowing more than one language are well known in Europe and Canada, where cultural communities speak different languages but enjoy equal status.

CBLT programs for majority-language students are not seen as compensatory education. Instead, they are considered enrichment programs that can provide something extra. In all these programs, students receive some of their instruction through their L1, which is always treated as an important part of both their education and their identity.

Content and Language Integrated Learning (CLIL)

CBLT is sometimes implemented by teaching one or two academic subjects in a foreign language. In Europe, this approach has been called **Content and Language Integrated Learning** (CLIL). According to Coyle, Hood, & Marsh (2010), CLIL 'is neither language learning nor subject learning, but an amalgam of both' (p. 4). Typically, these classes are offered to students at the secondary level who have already had and continue to have most of their instruction in their L1. Most will also have had a few hours a week of instruction in the foreign language, sometimes throughout their elementary school years. For example, a school in Germany might offer 14-year old students a science or history class in English, in addition to their class in English as a foreign language.

Although CLIL is a relatively new approach to foreign language education, it is now widely implemented. It is intended to increase the amount of time students spend in learning the foreign language while also preparing them to continue using the language in the wider community. This approach responds to the increased integration of the European community and the desire to equip young people with the language skills needed to move easily from country to country for work, personal enrichment, and for further studies abroad (Dalton-Puffer, 2011).

European implementations of CLIL have been studied by a number of researchers who have asked many questions about appropriate pedagogy, the preparation of teachers, and the challenges of integrating language and content (Coyle & Baetens Beardsmore, 2007; deGraaff, Koopman, & Westoff, 2007; Muñoz, 2007a). The outcomes have generally been very encouraging, but the great variety of implementations in many different countries means that more research is needed before general conclusions can safely be reached (Pérez-Cañado, 2012). Because the programs are implemented mainly at the secondary school level, there is an element of selectivity, as students usually have the option of continuing regular foreign language instruction or participating in a CLIL program that may be seen as more demanding (Bruton, 2011). Nevertheless, Lasagabaster (2008) cites research in German-speaking countries by Dalton-Puffer showing that, while academically talented students may reach high levels of foreign language skill in regular foreign language instruction, the CLIL approach allows students with average ability to achieve higher levels of skill than they have typically attained in traditional classes.

In the Asia-Pacific region, instruction in English as a foreign language is sometimes supplemented by English-language instruction in a number of school subjects. For example, in Hong Kong, instruction through English has long been part of the educational experience. Indeed, for many years, English was the medium of instruction for most students in secondary schools. This policy was challenged as more students gained access to secondary education, and after the return of Hong Kong from British to Chinese authority, there was a greater emphasis on education through students' L1, Cantonese. Researchers argued that, for most students, content learning was improved by the availability of L1 instruction (Marsh, Hau, & Kong, 2000). Nevertheless, there remains a strong desire for the development of proficiency in English. English immersion programs (see below) have been offered in both elementary and secondary schools (Hoare & Kong, 2008), but CBLT has also been implemented through the teaching of one or two subjects in English in Hong Kong and, more recently, in mainland China (Hoare, 2010).

In 2003, Malaysia adopted a policy of teaching mathematics and science in English to secondary school students. However, in 2009 the decision was made to return to teaching these subjects in Bahasa Malaysia (Malay) due to concerns about how effectively this implementation of CBLT prepared students for examinations (Gooch, 2009). In these settings and in others, it is often difficult to find teachers who have the combination of adequate L2 proficiency, specialized subject matter knowledge, and training in foreign-language pedagogy.

In most Canadian provinces, English-speaking students begin studying French at the age of nine or ten, and the instruction is typically offered for a few hours a week over a period of five to eight years. This instructional approach is referred to as **core French**, and for most English-speaking Canadians outside the province of Quebec, this continues to be the predominant approach to teaching French. In a number of schools, however, parents and educators have sought to increase the time students spend learning and using French by offering one or two academic courses in French as a supplement to the core French instruction. This is referred to as **extended French** and is typically offered at the late primary or secondary level (Swain, 1981a).

Immersion

The approach to CBLT that we will refer to as **immersion** has been widely implemented, and extensively studied for decades. Many immersion programs are based on a Canadian French immersion model that began as an educational experiment in a suburb of Montreal in the province of Quebec in the 1960s. English is the language spoken by the majority of Canadians, but French is the L1 of some 80 percent of the population of Quebec. A group of English-speaking parents sought a way to ensure that their children would have a level of French-language skill that would allow them to thrive in Quebec. The original model placed English-speaking kindergarten children in a class with a French-speaking teacher who addressed them only in French. As the students moved up through the grades, instruction in English was introduced into the curriculum, but most of their content subjects were taught in French throughout the elementary school years (Lambert & Tucker, 1972).

The French immersion approach that began in Quebec was soon adopted in other Canadian provinces. Over time, the approach was adapted to different settings and has evolved to include several different program types. As in the original program, some early total immersion programs place students in French instruction from the time they enter kindergarten and they do not start receiving instruction in English until as late as Grade 4. In these early total immersion programs, children are taught to read first in their L2. In some partial immersion programs, students have their early schooling, including initial **literacy** instruction in English, their L1. Students in these partial immersion programs will typically also have French lessons each day, with instruction that emphasizes oral comprehension and interaction. Immersion, in the form of subject matter instruction in French, is implemented when they are nine or ten years old. Other partial immersion programs provide instruction in both languages from the beginning of primary school, in roughly equal numbers of minutes. There are also late immersion models in which students do not experience CBLT instruction in their L2 until they reach late primary or early secondary school, having studied in core French programs for a few hours a week until then (see Genesee, 1987).

All the Canadian immersion programs share several characteristics. Nearly all students speak English, either because it is their L1 or because they have learned it as a second language in the wider community. Over a period of several years, they get a substantial amount of their subject matter instruction in French, and this instruction is delivered by bilingual teachers who take into account the status of their students as L2 learners. Teachers address the students in French but they usually understand when students speak English, and there is a range of tolerance for the students' use of English during French instruction. All immersion programs include some subject matter and language arts instruction in English, and students are expected to reach levels of achievement in English and in academic subject matter that are comparable to those achieved by English-speaking students who receive all their instruction in English (Swain & Lapkin, 1982).

The number of research reports on Canadian French immersion programs is impressive. These include evaluations carried out by local school boards and provincial ministries of education as well as studies by university researchers. The research has confirmed the finding of the earliest evaluations. Students achieve success in subject-matter learning. Their English language skills are comparable to those of students who have had their education in English, and they maintain their identity as English Canadians and continue to see themselves as primarily English speakers. They achieve high levels of comprehension in French and can express themselves both orally and in writing on topics related to academic subject matter. However, there are gaps in grammatical accuracy, lexical precision, and pragmatic appropriateness in their French, even after several years of CBLT in French immersion classes (Genesee, 2004; Lyster, 2007).

Over the years, some observers have focused on the limitations in French immersion students' ability to speak and write French correctly (Bibeau, 1982; Spilka, 1976), and it is widely understood that unless they interact with French speakers outside the school setting, the proficiency of French immersion students will be incomplete in some ways (Lyster, 2011). Nonetheless, there is strong support among Canadian parents and educators, who see this approach as more effective than any other for teaching French to Canadian Anglophones, especially those living in areas of the country where English is the majority language (Genesee, 1987; Stern, 1984).

As the Canadian population has changed, the makeup of student groups has also changed, and more students in French immersion come from families where languages other than English are spoken (Swain & Lapkin, 2005). In general, these programs have also been successful for them and, as a rule, students also achieve proficiency in English. In Quebec, there have been changes in language laws and policies since the first immersion programs were implemented, making French more prominent in public life in Montreal than it was in the 1960s. French language skills are now essential for many kinds of employment. Students from immigrant families, regardless of their L1, are now required to attend French language schools rather than the English language schools that house French immersion programs. Thus, rather than learning French in immersion classes in English language schools, they are integrated into French schools.

In recent census reports, Montreal's young Anglophones report the highest rate of French–English bilingualism in Canada, with nearly 80 percent saying that they feel comfortable using their L2 in daily life (Lightbown, 2012). This is quite a change from the patterns of Anglophone monolingualism in previous generations. It has been supported by the widespread adoption of immersion education for the English-speaking population as well as by the increased need and opportunity for both Canadian Anglophones and immigrants to use French outside the classroom.

Immersion education based on the Canadian models has been implemented in other countries, from Australia (de Courcy, 2002) to the USA (Fortune, Tedick, & Walker, 2008). By the end of 2011, the website of the Center for Applied Linguistics listed some 450 immersion programs in the USA. Nearly half were Spanish immersion programs, but there were also substantial numbers of programs in French and Mandarin, as well as smaller numbers of programs provided in other languages. A collection of research reports published by Johnson & Swain (1997) outlined the characteristics of immersion programs around the world as well as some of the ways in which they have been adapted according to local conditions and resources. For example, while all immersion programs include CBLT, the expectations for students' proficiency in the L2 varies among them. Tedick, Christian, & Fortune (2011) bring together reports on immersion in the USA and in several other countries, updating and extending the research reported in the 1997 Johnson & Swain collection.

Some researchers have pointed out how traditional immersion instruction, where the L2 is used only or primarily as a tool for academic discourse, can lead to students not knowing how to speak the informal language of their age peers (Tarone & Swain, 1995). One important innovation that can provide students with a more varied exposure to age-appropriate social uses of the language is the **dual immersion** approach that will be described on page 24.

The European Schools

The European Schools are a network of schools in a number of countries in the European Union (Baetens Beardsmore, 1993). Like the French immersion programs in Canada, the idea for the schools came from parents, in this case, parents who were working outside their home country and wanted to ensure that their children got both continuity in their L1 education and opportunities to learn other European languages. In these schools, students receive their initial literacy training and a substantial portion of their subject matter education in their L1. In addition, all students are taught an L2 throughout primary and secondary levels. As they advance through the grades, some of their academic content courses are also taught in their L2. The first L2 taught to all students is either English, French, or German, the major working languages of the European Union. However, the number of L1 backgrounds of children in these schools represents about a dozen languages, including Dutch, Italian, and Swedish.

In early primary school, the L2 is taught as a subject in one period a day, typically using a communicative approach with an emphasis on speaking and listening. From the third year of primary school (age 8+) the L2 is also gradually introduced in CBLT classes, where students from different L1 backgrounds are mixed together for 'European Hours' and for another school subject. For example, German L1 students whose L2 is French might join an English L1 group whose L2 is also French for a physical education class in French. At the secondary school level, students continue to study the L2 as a subject, in classes that include a focus on the study of grammar and vocabulary learning. In addition, students may take as many as half their subject matter courses in the L2 (Housen, Schoonjans, Janssens, Welcomme, Schoonheere, & Pierrard, 2011). Eventually, students also study a third language.

Some students in European Schools have opportunities to use their L2 outside the classroom, for example, a French L1/German L2 student whose parents are living and working in Germany. Other students attend European Schools in their home country and thus experience learning their L2 essentially as a foreign language. In most cases, however, students will have part of the L2 learning experience with students from other L1 groups. In all cases, students begin their schooling in their L1 and add other languages as they progress through the grades. Although the schools are public and seek to be inclusive, they have a reputation as being somewhat elitist and placing the greatest emphasis on academic achievement. This is perhaps reinforced by the fact that students who do not meet the high academic standards set in the secondary school may be held back or dismissed from the school, leaving a student population that may reflect a special group.

Unlike the original Canadian French immersion programs and many foreign language immersion programs in the USA, the European Schools are organized on the principle of starting children's education in their L1 and adding L2 over time, first through **direct instruction** and later through CBLT. In this sense, the European Schools are more like the partial immersion or late immersion programs that have been implemented in Canada. Nevertheless, in both North American immersion programs and the European Schools, the first concern is academic performance, and in all cases the students' L1 is valued and supported.

In comparing the learning outcomes in the European Schools to those in other programs that are based primarily on CBLT, one is struck by the very high levels of proficiency students attain in both content knowledge and L2 proficiency (Housen et al., 2011). In addition to the possible effects of selectivity of the student population that was mentioned above, the reasons for the favorable outcomes may include several factors, and research has touched on a number of them. In Chapters 3 and 4, we will look at some of this research, including studies of the impact of the language spoken in the wider community, the relative importance of language distance (for example, is English harder for Greek speakers than for Dutch speakers?), and the importance attached to including a structure-based component in students' L2 learning.

CBLT for Minority-Language Students

CBLT for minority-language students is different from CBLT for majority-language students in several important ways. Perhaps the most significant difference is that, for minority-language students, learning a new language and being educated in that language is *not optional*. It is a necessity if students are to receive an education that allows them to participate fully in the social and economic life of the wider community in which they live. Furthermore, whereas L2 programs for majority-language students are likely to be seen as essentially 'educational' matters, the L2 development of minority-language students is often entangled with social and political views and the opinions of people without professional experience in education. One of the most contentious aspects of education for minority-language students is the extent to which their L1 should be used as a medium of instruction during any part of their education in the majority-language system.

The challenges of educating minority-language students are being faced in many countries around the world—in countries of immigration such as Australia, Canada, France, Germany, the United Kingdom, and the USA, as well as in countries with populations of indigenous students who do not speak the majority or official language at home, such as Bolivia and Peru; this challenge also applies to parts of Australia, Canada, and the USA. While many local issues distinguish the different contexts, there are also many common challenges.

In the discussion below, for the sake of simplicity, I will use some of the terminology developed for the teaching and learning of English in the USA. Thus, for example, in discussing education for minority-language students, I will refer to '**English language learners**' (ELLs), to 'English as a second language' (ESL), and to 'English as the majority language', except when referring to a specific program in a place where another language predominates.

Submersion/Mainstream

The provision of content-based instruction that is appropriate to the needs of ELLs has been the subject of research, professional development, and curriculum planning for many years (Crandall, 1987; Kaufman & Crandall, 2005; Mohan, 1986; Snow, 1998; Snow & Brinton, 1997). As the number of ELLs continues to grow, the importance of ensuring that students can move forward with academic content while they learn English has become the concern of thousands of educators.

Not long after the first reports of the success of Canadian French immersion programs began to be published, Cohen & Swain (1976) and others expressed concern about the application of findings from those programs to the education of minority-language students in the USA. They emphasized the fact that Canadian French immersion was a voluntary program, designed to enrich the educational opportunities of majority-language children whose L1 remained an important element in their education. In their view, it could not be used as justification for educating minority-language children through English-only instruction. They distinguished between immersion and **submersion**, with the latter term referring to the situation in which children are in classrooms where almost everyone else—not only the teacher but also the other students—is already proficient in the language they are learning and where there is little recognition of the language students have learned outside school.

In **mainstream** classrooms, students who are second-language learners may get some individual help from their teacher or some instruction in separate **pull-out classes**, or they may have special teachers or teachers' aides who work with them in their regular classroom (sometimes called **push-in** assistance), but most of their subject matter instruction is provided in lessons designed to meet the needs of proficient speakers rather than of language learners. This is very different from the immersion model developed in Canada that we described above.

There is no doubt that some L2 learners have managed to thrive in mainstream classrooms in the USA and elsewhere. However, placing L2 students in mainstream classes without adequate support often leaves them far behind, unable to keep up with subject matter learning as their classmates continue to move forward. A too-frequent result is that ELLs are seen as somehow deficient or unable to learn. School systems that are designed for English speakers may not assess minority-language students in their L1. This could be because of legal limitations on the use of other languages or it may be the practical problem that assessment resources are not available in the students' L1, especially in schools where there are students from many different language backgrounds. Nevertheless, poor academic performance may reflect students' language proficiency rather than their content knowledge or their academic potential, and it has often been difficult to determine whether minority-language students who have difficulty in mainstream classrooms are dealing with problems that stem from their status as language learners or from a learning disability, **specific language impairment**, or from a neurological or developmental disability. As a result, minority-language students tend to be over-represented in special education classes and this may limit their opportunities for continued academic progress (Cummins, 1984).

In Chapters 3 and 4, we will look at some of the research on students' language and content learning in a variety of educational settings. We will see that, while there are many ways of providing instruction for ELLs, educational programs that respect the students' L1 knowledge and identity and give them special consideration as language learners are more effective than those in which students are left to sink or swim in the mainstream.

Sheltered Content Instruction

Sheltered content instruction is an approach to teaching ELLs that focuses on ensuring that they can understand academic content taught in English. Teachers present subject matter using pedagogical techniques that are intended to meet the needs of second language learners, for example, using more repetition and more demonstration than they might in a class without ELLs (Echevarria, Vogt, & Short, 2012). This approach emphasizes the importance of providing instruction that does not require L2 students to sink or swim but instead gives them the kind of support that allows them to access the grade-level content in the language they are still learning.

Sometimes sheltered content instruction is part of a **bilingual education** program, in which some subject matter instruction is provided in the students' L1. In other cases, sheltered instruction may be offered in separate classes for ELLs who are otherwise integrated into the mainstream with students whose L1 is the school language. Such classes are usually taught by content-area teachers who need to learn how to respond to the special learning needs of ELLs. Thus, an important aspect of sheltered content instruction is the emphasis on providing professional development to content-area teachers whose experience has been mainly with L1 students in mainstream classes. Several studies have shown how the approach can be enhanced by ensuring that teachers are well prepared for its implementation (Short, Echevarria, & Richards-Tutor, 2011).

Bilingual Education

The most straightforward definition of bilingual education is simply that it is an approach that provides instruction in two languages. Thus, the CBLT approaches for majority-language students described above are bilingual education programs because students always receive instruction in both L1 and L2. However, it would be wrong to assume, as some do, that all programs that are called 'bilingual' give equal status to L1 and L2 or that the goals for students' development of both languages are the same (Lessow-Hurley, 2013).

In the USA, the term 'bilingual education' has been used in reference to a great range of instructional approaches that vary widely in the amount of time devoted to each language. In *transitional* bilingual education, students may spend a few months or even a year or two receiving instruction through their L1, with the goal of moving them as soon as possible into English-only instruction. In *developmental* or late-exit bilingual education, students continue to receive instruction in the minority language for a longer period, and the programs are intended to help students develop their literacy and **academic language** abilities in both languages.

A review of research on students' academic achievement led Lindholm-Leary & Borsato (2006) to conclude that any program that takes account of ELLs' special needs as second language users is better than submersion in the mainstream and that in general, bilingual programs that include longer periods in students' L1 are better than those which make a rapid transition to English. They also caution, however, that asking 'Which program is best for ELLs?' will not result in satisfactory answers because, being "overly simplistic … it assumes that only one approach is the best for all students under all circumstances" (Lindholm-Leary & Borsato, 2006, p. 205).

In the 1960s and 1970s, support grew for bilingual education in the USA. Following many evaluations, evidence mounted that such programs were beneficial for minority-language children (Hakuta, 1986; Thomas & Collier, 2003). Like any widely implemented approach to education, this one was more successful in some places than in others. Furthermore, as bilingual education expanded to include more students, it was not always possible to ensure that the best practices were followed or that fully qualified professionals were available to staff all classes. There were also conflicting beliefs about the importance of L1 instruction and widely differing expectations about how long it should take for minority-language students to become proficient in the L2. A wave of harsh criticism of bilingual education began to appear in public debate, often on the basis of incorrect or misleading interpretations of information about how the programs were working. Some researchers and politicians condemned bilingual education as a failure that held students back from full success in the English-speaking community (Rossel & Baker, 1996; Unz, 1997).

Controversy surrounding bilingual education programs in the USA was especially highly charged in the late 1990s and by 2010, the attacks had successfully eroded support for it in many states. Crawford (2008) reviews many aspects of this controversy. Of greatest concern is that several states that had experienced considerable success with bilingual education found themselves unable to continue the programs after laws were passed, sometimes on the basis of state-wide referenda, prohibiting or restricting the use of languages other than English in classroom instruction.

As Lindholm-Leary & Borsato (2006) have suggested, there may be no single instructional approach that is always best for minority-language students in majority-language school systems. Nevertheless, the prohibition of bilingual education programs took away one of the options that had worked well for many students. There is little evidence that this has improved educational outcomes for ELLs, and it has effectively prevented thousands of students from developing academic language and literacy skills in their L1. This in itself represents a lost resource for children and their families, as well as for the wider community.

Structured English Immersion

Structured English immersion (SEI) is not CBLT. Thus, in spite of the similarity in the name, it is not like the immersion programs for majority-language students described above. Rather, it is a program to teach students English in order to prepare them to learn academic content in the mainstream. In some US states, SEI has become the only approach that is sanctioned by educational authorities. Other approaches, including bilingual education, have been discontinued, either by administrative decisions or, in several states, by ballot initiatives that invited the public to determine how ELLs should be taught.

In SEI, the goal is to teach English intensively so that students become proficient in the language as quickly as possible. The expectation is that most students will be able to transition to the mainstream within a year. During the period of SEI, there may some content-based instruction, but the emphasis is on learning the language itself, with the understanding that students are being prepared for integration into mainstream classes where they will receive content-based instruction.

The SEI approach has sparked a great deal of controversy from researchers and educators who see the process and outcomes very differently. Supporters urge the adoption of this approach, based on their understanding of foreign language instruction. Students are explicitly and systematically taught pronunciation, vocabulary, and grammar, as well as English reading and writing. Some subject matter is taught, using materials designed for L2 learners, but the emphasis is on developing English language skills that are adequate for full participation in the mainstream. Proponents of this approach argue that students cannot benefit from CBLT in the mainstream before their English skills have reached a certain level and that SEI leads to more rapid acquisition of English by focusing on teaching *English* rather than teaching *in English* (Clark, 2009).

Critics of SEI assert that the approach is not based on evidence from research on how languages are acquired and how long it takes for students to become proficient in their L2. Some critics also express concern about the stigmatizing or isolating effects of placing students in separate SEI classes while they are learning English. They argue that such separation of students from their peers may result in problems with their integration into the regular school programs. They also point to research showing that continuing L1 development is more effective than SEI and that programs providing long term bilingual instruction ultimately lead to the best outcomes, not only for content learning but also for English language learning (Krashen, Rolstad, & MacSwan, 2007).

The controversy over SEI as an alternative to CBLT, including bilingual education, has been heated and the heat has been fueled by political as well as educational opinions. As with many such controversies, those on each side seem so deeply convinced of the wisdom of their view that alternatives or even compromise solutions that provide both intensive English instruction and bilingual education seem to be excluded. And yet, there is reason to believe that elements from the two approaches could be integrated into a balanced instructional program.

Dual Immersion

In school jurisdictions in several US states where bilingual education has been disallowed, an exception has been made for what is referred to as dual immersion or two-way instruction. In this educational model, minority- and majority-language students are taught their academic subjects in both their L1 and their L2. This approach has received considerable attention from educators and researchers (Calderón & Minaya-Rowe, 2003; deJong & Howard, 2009; Lindholm-Leary, 2001).

There are several models of dual immersion in US schools (Howard, Sugarman, & Christian, 2003). The instructional model that is chosen in a given location depends partly on whether there is a large population of students from the minority-language group. Where there are enough students who speak each language, classes can be made up of an equal number from each language group and half the instruction can be offered in English and half in the minority-group students' L1. In settings where there are fewer speakers of the minority language, the instruction may be offered primarily in the minority language for the first few years, with instruction in the majority language gradually being added as students grow older—in a pattern similar to that of the original early French immersion programs (Lindholm-Leary, 2011).

As in Canadian-type immersion and in European School models, the long-term goal of dual immersion programs is to promote academic language and literacy in both students' L1 and their L2. In addition, this kind of dual immersion program can provide students with greater opportunities to interact with peers who are fluent speakers of their second language, whether that language is the minority or majority language in the community. Such **peer interaction** may increase motivation to learn and also provide access to age-appropriate social language as well as academic language.

The dual immersion approach resembles the European Schools model in the sense that it provides opportunities for students from different backgrounds to learn each other's languages while also continuing to develop age-appropriate academic proficiency in their L1. On the other hand, in contrast to the European Schools context, dual immersion programs often exist in settings where there is a substantial difference in the perceived status of the two languages and their speakers in the community. This is not always the case, however, as illustrated by the research on Chinese–English dual immersion classes (Lindholm-Leary, 2011). Research has provided strong support for this way of educating children (Collier & Thomas, 2004).

CBLT in Post-Colonial Settings

In many countries, CBLT has been a fact of life for decades—or even centuries—as education has been offered in schools set up by colonizers or by those who held the political power and resources in countries where substantial populations of citizens speak different languages. In this situation, the terms 'minority' and 'majority' language do not have the same meaning as they have in the situations described above. In these situations, the students speak one or more of the community languages that are spoken by the vast majority of the population. Nevertheless, for historical reasons, some or all of their education has been available only in another language, often the language of a former colonizing country.

For generations, students have been educated in schools where a European language—English, French, Portuguese, Spanish—is the medium of instruction, even though students often arrive at school with little or no knowledge of that language (Benson, 2004). Such policies reflect a number of challenges faced by education systems in post-colonial settings. In some countries, the choice of language is based on the need to provide a unifying education that does not favor one cultural group over another, for example, in India and in a number of African countries. In other cases, education officials and parents may fear that local languages will not lead to opportunities for further education and jobs (Chimbutane, 2011; Obondo, 2007). In many places, there is a lack of trained teachers and academic materials for local languages.

Parents and local officials are often suspicious of suggestions that using local languages at school can be a good foundation for learning the high-status colonial language, even though research has shown this to be true in other contexts and even in some African schools (Tembe & Norton, 2008). As Benson (2004) observes:

> The elite inevitably speak the prestige code, which is usually the language of the former colonizing power and the 'official' language of governance and schooling; meanwhile, other groups speak languages that often lack formal recognition, and their access to the prestige language is limited even if they themselves make up a numerical majority of the population.
>
> (Benson, 2004, p. 49)

In Latin America, many students who speak indigenous languages at home receive their schooling in Portuguese or Spanish (Hornberger, 2002). Even when early education is offered in local or regional languages, secondary education may be offered only in Portuguese or Spanish, and students who go on to higher education find that university lectures and textbooks are available only in these languages. As noted in the section on immersion approaches, English has been a significant presence in secondary- and post-secondary education in some parts of Asia, even where local languages are used in primary school classes (Johnson & Swain, 1997).

The outcomes of education through high prestige languages in post-colonial settings have varied greatly. In some countries, especially those with limited resources for educational infrastructure and professional development of teachers, overall levels of literacy and academic achievement are very low. In others, students perform at the highest levels on measures such as the PISA (Program for International Student Assessment) tests, confirming that factors other than language of instruction affect educational achievement.

Activity 1.2

The table on page 28 lists eight ways of teaching L2 learners and eight important features of instruction. Match each teaching approach with its characteristic features. In some cases, the match will involve a simple *yes/no*. In other cases, the matching is more complicated and will require an 'it depends' response. Complete the table as a way of reflecting on your understanding of the different approaches to CBLT.

Pedagogical Practice in CBLT

CBLT is implemented in a great variety of situations and with the use of a great variety of pedagogical practices in the context of different educational philosophies. Researchers have carried out both qualitative and quantitative observational studies and have reported seeing a range of instructional approaches. Some classes are characterized by traditional *transmission* models of instruction. In this type of instruction, the teacher provides information through lectures or demonstrations while students take notes or answer teachers' questions in a classic *IRE* pattern (the teacher *initiates* an interaction by asking a question; a student *responds*; the teacher then *evaluates* the student's response). Other classes reflect *discovery learning*

	Foreign language immersion	Transitional bilingual education	Developmental bilingual education	CLIL/ European Schools	Dual immersion	Sheltered content instruction	Structured English immersion	Mainstream classroom
Age- or grade-appropriate content instruction								
Instruction adapted for L2 learners								
Interaction with L2 peers								
Direct instruction in L2								
Support for L1 literacy								
L2 instruction beginning from Pre-K or K								
L1 and L2 have equal status in community								
Intended primarily for minority- language students								

Table 1.1 Approaches to teaching language and content

approaches that involve learners in searching for information. In this approach, teachers seek to encourage longer student responses, requiring more reflection and risk-taking. This kind of instruction often places students in contexts where they interact with other students in pairs or groups for **cooperative learning**. Many classes include activities that reflect both traditional teacher-centered and more collaborative interaction. Each approach has been found important in preparing students for success in a variety of educational settings.

The common thread in the varied implementations of CBLT is the dual goal of learning academic content that is challenging and age-appropriate while at the same time learning the second or foreign language in which that subject matter is taught.

Learning the Language and Learning the Content

The shared assumption of CBLT programs is that language and content can be learned at the same time, but there is a range of practical organizational structures for providing instruction that covers both. That range goes from offering language instruction in a class that is separate from content classes to a fully integrated organization in which one teacher is expected to ensure that students learn the content and that they also continue to develop greater sophistication, accuracy, and fluency in the new language. Classroom Snapshots 1.1 and 1.2 represent the two approaches. The teacher in Classroom Snapshot 1.1 is teaching a separate lesson that is meant to focus on students' English skills; in Classroom Snapshot 1.2, the students are learning language as they learn mathematics, with an emphasis on language as the vehicle for subject-matter learning.

One approach to offering separate **language-focused instruction** for students in mainstream education is to provide pull-out instruction (see Collier, 1995). This approach takes students out of their content lessons for part of the school day. The decision to work this way may be related to the lack of preparation that content teachers feel they have for teaching language. Some generalist elementary school teachers and some specialists who have been trained to teach science, history, or mathematics at the secondary level prefer to have a trained language teacher provide language-focused instruction. However, unless there is close coordination between the language and content teachers, the features of language that are focused on in the language class are often not the ones that students need to use in their content classes.

Sometimes, even the same teacher may teach vocabulary and grammar in the language arts class as if it were unrelated to the activities that students engage in during content classes. In immersion settings, the same teacher may teach both language-focused and content-focused lessons, but limit the focus on language to the language arts classes (Fazio & Lyster, 1998). Educators may believe that students should focus on science or mathematics while they are in the science or mathematics class, reserving the focus on language for a separate lesson. Such separation may deprive students of opportunities to focus on specific features of language at the very moment when their motivation to learn them may be at its highest (Lightbown, 1998).

Lyster (2007) cites Swain & Carroll's (1987) observation that in French immersion classes, it was "relatively rare for teachers to (a) refer during content-based lessons to what had been presented in a grammar lesson and (b) to set up content-based activities specifically to focus on form related to meaning" (Lyster, 2007 pp. 26–7). They tended "to avoid language issues during content-based instruction and instead to wait for language arts lessons to address language structure in relatively traditional ways" (p. 27). Thus, students spent considerable time in language arts classes doing exercises on language features that were not related to the linguistic challenges that were present in their content classes.

In Chapter 2, we will see that what is learned in one setting may be more difficult to retrieve in another, where the context and the cognitive processes are different. That is, learning grammar rules in a grammar class may result in knowledge that is not easily transferable to the content classroom where there are competing demands for cognitive processing. Thus aspects of grammar that may seem to have been learned when a test was given in the grammar class are the source of ongoing errors in the content class.

This situation of separating language and content seems to have arisen in part because content teachers often feel, quite understandably, that they do not know how to teach language. Their focus is on ensuring that students learn the content, and they see time spent focusing on language as time away from the content. In addition, the view that language acquisition can take place 'incidentally' while students' attention is turned toward the content has been widely expressed in the CBLT literature, based in part on interpretations of language acquisition research which does indeed show, as we will see in Chapter 2, that much language is acquired incidentally. However, evidence from language acquisition research in school settings, including CBLT and other kinds of communicative language teaching, has shown that more systematic and intentional focus on language itself is an important—probably essential—element for ensuring that language development goes beyond basic levels (Genesee, 1987; Lyster, 2007).

Language for Academic and Social Purposes

In some CBLT contexts, students are expected to acquire content and language with very little explicit attention to the language itself. This is the case for many students plunged into mainstream classes where there are few second language learners and thus no organized plan or program to meet their needs. In immersion programs, teachers may feel that adapting their instruction so that students can understand the content is sufficient for fostering language acquisition.

The absence of language-focused instruction has also been observed in transitional bilingual education programs where, having had a brief period of content instruction (possibly including initial literacy) in L1 combined with some specific L2 instruction, students are deemed to have reached a level of proficiency that no longer requires any special focus on language. In these situations, teachers will often describe students as 'fluent' and may assume that any difficulties they have in academic work are related to lack of motivation, poor work habits, low ability, or even a developmental or learning disability (Cummins, 1984).

The difficulty teachers have in distinguishing students' language-based limitations from other types of problems can be explained in part in terms of two kinds of language proficiency—the informal language needed for social interaction with peers and the more formal language needed for understanding and producing academic texts (both oral and written). We will discuss this further in Chapter 2 and we will see some of the ways these two kinds of language proficiency are developed in different programs when we look at classroom-based research in Chapters 3 and 4.

Who teaches?

Some CBLT classes are taught by teachers who have experience in teaching a particular age group or a particular subject matter, but who have little experience or training for teaching second language learners, for example, when a high school history teacher has English language learners (ELLs) in his or her class for the first time or when a first grade teacher must guide the first literacy experiences of a child who does not yet speak the language. In other cases, teachers may have a background in second language teaching but little preparation for teaching mathematics, science, or social studies—for example, when a teacher trained to teach English as a foreign language (EFL) is assigned to teach biology in English to students in a CLIL class in Germany. And in some cases, teachers with subject matter expertise are recruited to teach CBLT classes in a language in which their own proficiency is limited, such as when a Malaysian mathematics teacher must teach a familiar subject matter in English, a less familiar language.

CBLT is based on the expectation that students can learn language and content at the same time. Interestingly, there seems to be less consensus about whether a single teacher *can* teach language and content at the same time. Observation of classes taught by teachers with pedagogical training in content areas (but not second language teaching) show that they may sometimes fail to see students' difficulties as being language-based. On the other hand, teachers with second language training but little background in the academic content of a particular subject matter may focus on basic communication skills, not realizing that students are not acquiring the kind of language that is required for more advanced study in that academic content (Kong & Hoare, 2011).

Without training to help them understand the different language requirements for academic and social purposes, teachers who see students interact with their friends and participate during classroom oral interaction may conclude that the language itself is not a problem. This may lead them to conclude that any academic problems are due to students' inability to understand the subject matter or to their lack of interest and motivation in the academic work. The difficulty of distinguishing between academic problems that are due to individual disabilities rather than a lack of language proficiency can lead to students being directed into remediation programs that do not correspond to their real needs (Cummins, 1984; Fortune, 2010; Kohnert, 2007).

One approach that has proven effective in CBLT is professional development that shows teachers how to plan and implement each lesson with *both* language *and* content objectives (Echevarria et al., 2012). Another kind of professional development, based on systemic functional linguistics, has also enabled teachers to understand and help students understand how language and meaning are interrelated (Schleppegrell, 2004). Many scholars and teachers have collaborated in efforts to find the right balance for ensuring that students can learn both content and language (Snow, Met, & Genesee, 1989). In Chapters 3 and 4, we will look at some studies that show how instruction and **corrective feedback** on language have—or have not—been integrated with academic content in elementary and secondary school CBLT classes.

Professional development may provide teachers with some pedagogical strategies that can help second language learners gain access to meaning in content classes (Short, Echevarria, & Richards-Tutor, 2011). Professional development can also help teachers recognize language-related problems. For example, most teachers are likely to notice if students produce work that includes overt errors such as subject–verb agreement. However, when students become more advanced, they still need support as they continue to develop their language proficiency. Teachers who do not have specific training for academic language use may find it hard to identify or even recognize gaps in students' language at these more advanced levels (Schleppegrell & O'Hallaron, 2011; Wong Fillmore & Snow, 2000).

One response to the difficulty a single teacher faces in having responsibility for both language and content is to have two teachers, one whose focus is on language and one whose focus is on content. Teemant, Bernhardt, & Rodríguez-Muñoz (1997) propose some very practical principles to guide collaboration between language teachers and content teachers. Among those principles are "content and language go hand in hand; concept and language gaps require different approaches; content should not be compromised or diluted" (pp. 312–13). The authors suggest that their principles can serve as a way to "encourage conversation" and "represent a starting point for focused and strategic collaboration [between ESL teachers] and content-area teachers" (p. 318). In observing the work of secondary school teachers in Australia, Arkoudis (2006) found that when the content teacher and the English language teacher spent time together outside the classroom, discussing and planning their respective lessons, they converged toward a more effective pedagogy, developing an understanding and appreciation of each other's expertise.

When language instruction is separate from the subject matter lessons, the greatest benefits will be achieved if the language instruction is coordinated with the content instruction, so that the language features students focus on in the language class prove to be useful to them when they are working in the content class. Successful coordination is by no means inevitable, however (Creese, 2005; Davison, 2006) and, as Arkoudis (2006) puts it, there is often "rough ground between ESL and mainstream teachers" who are expected to plan and carry out lessons that complement each other and give students the best of both kinds of expertise. As we have seen, even the same teacher may not see language and content lessons as related, thereby missing opportunities to focus language learning efforts on aspects of language that learners need in content-based lessons. We will return to this issue in Chapter 2, as we look at research on how we learn and how we can best remember what we have learned.

Activity 1.3

Compare the CBLT experiences of an English-speaking kindergarten child in a Canadian French immersion program and an immigrant child in a mainstream kindergarten class in the USA. Make a list of several similarities and several differences in their first year of CBLT. Now do the same for an English-speaking student starting a Grade 7 late French immersion program in Canada, a newly arrived 12-year-old immigrant from Poland, and another from Somalia entering a mainstream class in the USA. Organize your lists in terms of the roles of L1, prior educational experience, expectations within the L2 educational settings, and other factors that you think might affect outcomes for both L1 and L2 development for all these students.

Summary

In this chapter, you have been invited to reflect on what you already know about CBLT and how you think it can work in practice. We have described some of the ways CBLT has been implemented to serve the needs of both majority- and minority-language students around the world. We have begun to recognize some of the successes and challenges that different CBLT programs have experienced. In Chapter 2, we will emphasize some of the background research on learning and teaching academic content as well as language itself.

2 Learning Language and Learning Content

Preview

This chapter lays a foundation for looking at the research in CBLT classrooms that will be featured in Chapters 3 and 4. We begin by reviewing some research and theory about how language is learned and how content is learned through language. Some of the research was carried out with L2 learners in second/foreign language classrooms. Other studies took place in other contexts and were designed to investigate more general questions about second language acquisition, skill learning and performance, cognitive processing, and educational effectiveness.

We will look at what we know about human learning and how this knowledge relates to our expectations for CBLT. We will see that the kinds of language processing that take place in CBLT can offer valuable opportunities for students to acquire and retain both the new language and the academic subject matter. We will also see why there are times when it may be beneficial to focus on either language or content in order to achieve the greatest learning success for both. The chapter ends with the description of a pedagogical framework for ensuring that L2 learners have the variety of experience and instruction that is most likely to lead to success.

Second Language Acquisition

Countless research studies have investigated the cognitive and social aspects of learning a second language. Some studies have explored the effect of different learning experiences and practice opportunities in determining learners' eventual success. Other studies have focused on factors internal to the learner, such as age, first language, or linguistic aptitude. Many questions remain unanswered, but we have learned a great deal about how children and adults accomplish this challenging task. In the following pages, we will look at some of the important concepts that have emerged from this research, including the time it takes to learn a language and the conditions that are necessary for learning to continue.

The Importance of Time

Time is an important variable in language development, in terms of the total amount of time available for learning, the way that time is distributed, the age at which learning begins, and how long it continues.

Time on Task

An indisputable fact about language acquisition is that it takes time. Don't believe the internet ads that promise you can learn a language in 10 days! When children arrive at school, they have already spent thousands of hours hearing and speaking the language or languages of their environment. Typical foreign language programs offer a few hundred hours of exposure to the new language, often spread thinly over several years of classes. In countries where schools receive many immigrant children, people often believe that children should start learning the second language as early as possible in order to maximize the 'time on task' for learning the majority language. As we will see, researchers have concluded that it typically takes children several years to achieve age-appropriate ability to use language for academic purposes (Collier, 1987, 1989; Cummins, 2000). However, while time on task is a major factor in language learning, the 'common sense' belief in the effectiveness of spending as much time as possible in the L2 environment needs to be understood with considerably more subtlety and needs to be investigated systematically.

Research with language learners at school has shown repeatedly that helping children develop their L1 is an important part of promoting L2 skill, content knowledge, and general cognitive functioning. Cummins (1980) portrays the language proficiency of bilinguals in terms of an iceberg metaphor. An individual's observable use of first and second languages is represented by two 'tips' of a large iceberg. Most of the iceberg is underwater, and this large volume of the iceberg represents the 'common underlying language proficiency' that is the basis for the observable aspects of language use. The common underlying proficiency includes knowledge of both languages and Cummins argues persuasively that the languages are interdependent. Thus, strengthening one language can also strengthen the other.

The idea that time spent using the L1 prohibits or restricts the learning of the L2 has contributed to an educational culture where many minority-language children experience subtractive bilingualism, that is, where their L1 abilities decline as their L2 abilities increase. The research overwhelmingly supports **additive bilingualism**, where both the L1 and the L2 are respected and encouraged in education (Thomas & Collier, 2003).

That is, instruction in L1 followed by instruction in L2 or simultaneous instruction in L1 and L2 will be more effective for L2 knowledge and skill in the long term than education through the L2 alone. Goldenberg (2008) reports on a conversation that will be familiar to almost anyone who has had to explain the value of maintaining and developing students' L1:

> To some people this finding might seem counterintuitive. A few years ago a fair-minded colleague expressed disbelief: 'Doesn't it just make sense,' she asked, 'that the earlier and more intensively children are placed in all-English instruction at school the better their English achievement will eventually be?' That's when it hit me: when the goal is English proficiency, delivering any instruction in the first language probably does not make sense to some people. But this is why we do scientific research: common sense does not always turn out to be the truth. If we only relied on common sense, we would still think the sun revolves around a flat earth.
>
> (Goldenberg, 2008, p. 15)

Although time is not the only variable that affects outcomes, research makes it clear that sufficient time for learning is essential. In the classroom, time often seems to be a scarce resource, especially for students who are learning more than one language at school. For this reason, outcomes are enhanced when teachers engage in pedagogical practices that make the best use of the time available. In classroom interaction, time can be lost in lengthy 'transitions' between activities, periods during which students are expected to stand in line and be quiet or to wait patiently at their desks for the next instructional event. Transitional moments can be incorporated into effective pedagogy in many ways—by making sure students always have something to read or do during the quiet times at their desk, by having students engage in some guided conversation or even simple activities such as counting off or reciting some new learning as they are lining up. In the context of English language learners in US schools, Echevarria, et al. (2012) say it very well:

> English learners are the students who can least afford to have valuable time squandered through boredom, inattention, socializing, and other off-task behaviors. Time is also wasted when teachers are ill prepared; have poor classroom management skills; spend excessive amounts of time making announcements, passing out and handing in papers; and the like. The most effective teachers minimize these behaviors and maximize time spent actively engaged in instruction.
>
> (Echevarria et al., 2012, p. 195)

Students in any educational program need to make the best use of all the time they have, and they need to be encouraged to continue learning outside the classroom. Above all, teachers, parents, students, and policy makers need to understand that language learning requires a great deal of time. This does not mean that students' content learning should be 'put on hold' while they learn the language. Rather, educators should ensure that students continue to learn academic content through appropriate CBLT instruction and, where feasible, through their L1.

The Spacing Effect

Another way that time affects learning can be seen in the spacing effect (Bjork, 1994; Dempster, 1996). Numerous studies in both research laboratories and classrooms have reached a strong consensus that long-term learning is more likely to occur when learning and practice opportunities are spaced than when they are massed. In the most familiar terms, this is the finding that explains why a student can spend hours cramming for an examination, do well on the test, and then forget what was learned. More effective learning is achieved when learning and practice events are spaced over a longer time period, with periods of rest or other activity between the events.

Some studies of the spacing effect have been carried out in classroom lessons; others required participants to learn relatively simple material, such as lists of words. Learning that takes place over time has been shown to be more effective in almost every setting. Is some studies, it has also been found that learning outcomes are further enhanced if the material to be learned occurs in multiple contexts, with opportunities for using language in a variety of situations, engaging a variety of cognitive processes and language skills. This is most likely to happen if the learning opportunities are spread out over time.

One finding of research on foreign language learning in classrooms appears at first to contradict the spacing effect: students who experience a period of intensive foreign language instruction for several months appear to acquire better language abilities than those whose instruction is spread out over many years in half-hour or one-hour lessons, an approach sometimes referred to as 'drip feed' (Lightbown & Spada, 1991; Stern, 1985). There are a number of reasons for this. First, even though the intensive courses are not spread out as much as the drip-feed courses, they do tend to extend over periods of several months, creating many opportunities for students to review and recycle what they have learned. In addition, the total time available for instruction in typical drip-feed approaches rarely adds up to more than a few hundred hours throughout years of schooling. More intensive instruction, in addition to providing more hours of exposure to the language during each school day, usually adds more total time for learning as well (Collins et al., 1999). It is noteworthy, however, that the benefits of the more concentrated instruction are apparent even when students are assessed after the same total number of hours (Collins & White, 2011; Muñoz, 2006) or indeed even when the total time for instruction in compact courses adds up to fewer hours (Marshall, 2011).

One of the ways that compact and intensive instruction, including CBLT, promotes successful learning is by creating opportunities for students to engage in the kinds of projects and group-work activities that are very difficult to organize effectively in language classes that last 45 minutes or an hour. The evidence that students benefit from interacting with each other as well as with the teacher has been provided by research that has looked at learners from preschool to university. Collaborative work gives students opportunities to practice language use in ways that are simply impossible in a teacher-centered activity. We will return to this topic later in this chapter.

Motivation may also contribute to the success of compact and intensive courses. In drip-feed instruction, progress can seem very slow, and it is difficult for students to reach a level of ability or autonomy that would enable them to continue learning outside the classroom. If they feel that they have learned very little in instruction that adds up to scores rather than hundreds of hours in a year, they may lose their motivation to continue learning over the long term. As noted above, researchers have shown that, even when learning is measured after an equal number of hours, the students in the more intensive instruction do better. Foreign language instruction provided through compact or intensive courses, including that which is based on CBLT, leads to more rapid progress, and students retain their advantage over those in the drip-feed courses even if they return to those kinds of programs (Hawkins, 1988; Lightbown & Spada, 1991).

The Learner's Age

Another issue related to total time on task is the age at which L2 learning begins. The belief that 'younger is better' for second language learning is widely held, and there are some good reasons for that. Children who have substantial contact with a second language from earliest childhood and continue using the language as adolescents may indeed come to use the language fluently, using the same patterns of grammar and vocabulary as their peers who speak that language as their L1. However, an early start is no guarantee that students will acquire native-like skill (Lightbown, 2008a). To understand the role of age as a predictor in L2 success, it is important to look carefully at research that considers age together with other factors in explaining what it is that young learners do 'better' and what advantages there may be for older learners, especially in school settings (Muñoz, 2007b).

In the context of drip-feed foreign language instruction at school, where students continue to learn and use their first language as the main language for content learning, it is often the case that the total amount of time for learning the second language is quite limited. The age at which L2 instruction begins is often hard to separate from the total time spent learning, as well as the distribution of time. Learners who begin at an early age may accumulate more hours, thus making it hard to determine whether differences are due to their starting age or to the total number of instructional hours. Some researchers looking at foreign language instruction have teased these factors apart by studying learners' language development at the end of the same number of hours of instruction.

In the Barcelona Age Factor study, Muñoz (2006) and her colleagues found that an earlier start did not lead to greater success for Spanish–Catalan bilingual students learning English as a foreign language. Instead, on most measures, learners who started learning in the later years of primary schooling outperformed the younger learners who had accumulated the same number of hours. Muñoz attributed this benefit to older learners' ability to use their greater cognitive maturity for intentional learning while younger learners, dependent on incidental learning processes, needed more time to reach the same level. Cognitive maturity may have particular relevance for learning in CBLT settings where older students are better able to recognize the challenges they face and to learn strategies to help them reach their goals.

In immersion settings for majority-language students who have little contact with the L2 outside the classroom, the research has shown some benefits for an earlier start, although not all L2 skills are affected equally (Genesee, 1987). It is important to repeat, however, that these programs do not entail the loss of the students' L1, nor are they expected to achieve L2 proficiency that is native-like in all respects.

As we have seen, researchers have found that time spent in strengthening a child's L1 development, especially their literacy skills, has a positive impact on the long term development of the L2 (Goldenberg, 2008). It cannot be said often enough that no research supports the belief that the L2 will be learned faster and better if the L1 is forgotten. Instead, children from both minority and majority groups benefit from additive bilingualism. Furthermore, an earlier start that entails the loss of a child's first language can have other negative consequences, not only for the child's family relationships (Wong Fillmore, 2000) but also for the child's cognitive and academic growth (Cummins, 2000). Importantly, bilingualism that is additive and that involves the acquisition of literacy skills in both languages and the sustained use of both languages over time has been found to be associated with cognitive advantages throughout life (Bialystok, 2007).

Language Acquisition Processes

We turn now to a discussion of what we know about some of the processes involved in language acquisition by children and adolescents, whether in or out of the instructional setting.

Comprehensible Input

All language learning begins with a learner's ability to recognize some patterns and eventually to draw some meaning from the stream of speech or the sequence of letters or symbols in the new language. Any discussion of language acquisition must take into account the samples of the language that learners are exposed to—the input. Krashen's (1989) **comprehensible input hypothesis** expands this fundamental idea by proposing that the single most valuable resource for second language acquisition is the availability of comprehensible input—samples of the language that the learner understands. His hypothesis further specifies that, to promote language acquisition, the comprehensible input must also contain a modest number of new linguistic elements. Those new elements may include new vocabulary, new patterns for combining words, indicators of tense and number, or some other aspect of grammar.

Krashen's hypothesis is that, while learners are paying attention to the meaning carried by the comprehensible input, they are incidentally learning the elements of the language itself. Language acquisition researchers have confirmed that the human mind will indeed acquire a considerable amount of language while the listener/reader's focus is on meaning. This important understanding about language acquisition is reflected in CBLT in the many ways that teachers seek to make academic content language comprehensible to learners (Echevarria et al., 2012). It is understood that making the language comprehensible supports not just content knowledge but also language development.

The importance of comprehensible input can hardly be overstated, but it is not as simple as it seems. The details of how input shapes acquisition have been greatly refined and elaborated since the early days of the comprehensible input hypothesis. Let's look at some of the things we know about how input is related to language acquisition.

The comprehensibility of language input is affected by both contextual cues (for example, illustrations or gestures) and prior knowledge of a topic. Teachers often prepare students for a new unit (for example, a science unit on textiles) by providing illustrations or realia (for example, a box of different fabric samples) or encouraging students to brainstorm what they already know (for example, by asking them to identify the type of fabric in the clothing they are wearing or asking what they know about the source of cotton or wool). When they do this, they are reflecting the importance of creating situations in which students' comprehension is enhanced because they can make associations between the new information and an existing knowledge framework or schema.

Some of the most famous experiments showing the importance of prior knowledge were published in the 1970s by Bransford & Johnson. These cognitive psychologists were interested in how we learn and how we recall what we have learned. Their studies were carried out with groups of high school and university students. The results of these simple studies provide an excellent illustration of the importance of ensuring that students have some background knowledge or contextual information that will allow them to understand and learn from a story, a non-fiction text, a science lesson, or a conversation. One of their studies is described in Spotlight Study 2.1.

Spotlight Study 2.1

Fifty high school students heard the following paragraph read once. Before they heard it, they were told that they would be asked to recall as much as possible of what they had heard. After they heard it, they were asked to say how difficult they thought it was to understand and then to write down as many ideas from the passage as they could remember. Read the passage and think about how well you think you might do on the task. Better yet, read it to some friends and ask them whether they find it easy or difficult and how much they can remember about what they hear.

> The procedure is actually quite simple. First you arrange things into different groups. Of course, one pile may be sufficient depending on how much there is to do. If you have to go somewhere else due to lack of facilities that is the next step, otherwise you are pretty well set. It is important not to overdo things. That is, it is better to do too few things at once than too many. In the short run this may not seem important but complications can easily arise. A mistake can be expensive as well. At first the whole procedure will seem complicated.

Soon, however, it will become just another facet of life. It is difficult to foresee any end to the necessity for this task in the immediate future, but then one never can tell. After the procedure is completed one arranges the materials into different groups again. Then they can be put into their appropriate places. Eventually they will be used once more and the whole cycle will then have to be repeated. However, that is part of life.

(Bransford & Johnson, 1972, p. 722)

Some students found this task quite easy and remembered an average of almost six ideas from the text. Others found it difficult and remembered fewer than three ideas on average. What was the difference between the groups?

Students who found it easy to remember a number of ideas from this passage had been told, before listening, that the paragraph was about washing clothes. The other groups were either never told what the topic was or they were told the topic immediately after they had heard the text. It turned out that being told after the fact did not improve comprehension or recall. Prior knowledge of the topic allowed one group to recall what they already knew about doing laundry and to interpret what they heard within that schema. For those without the prior knowledge, even learning what the topic was immediately after hearing the passage was not enough to help them remember more of the details of what they had heard in the text. ■

What are some of the other factors besides prior knowledge and contextual cues that help to make language comprehensible and make input a source for language acquisition?

The frequency with which language features occur in the input is significant in determining what learners acquire (Ellis, 2002, 2009). For example, most conversational language uses and reuses the same one or two thousand words. Through hearing and participating in conversations, learners are likely to learn those words and phrases more easily than those that occur less frequently. In studies of language input available in second language classrooms, researchers have found that some language features that are common and frequent in language outside the classroom can be surprisingly rare or even absent in content-based lessons. We will see some examples of this in Chapters 3 and 4.

The issue of frequency is relevant not only to individual words or grammatical markers. Both spoken and written language input will also contain units that may be several words long. These formulaic units of language—sometimes called chunks—include routines such as 'What's that?' or 'Not right now' but also units such as 'as much as' or 'in addition to' that mix and match with other chunks in ways that are both creative and predictable (Bardovi-Harlig, 2009; Wray, 2000). Students whose L2 learning experience takes place mainly in foreign language classrooms know far fewer of these social routines than those who have spent time interacting with peers, for example, in study abroad programs (Roever, 2012). This suggests that instruction for foreign language learners—including those in CBLT—needs to increase students' exposure to those features of language that can substantially improve their ability to use the language in a variety of situations beyond the routines that are typical of classroom interaction.

Within the CBLT classroom, formulaic units are also important for academic language (Simpson-Vlach & Ellis, 2010). Hearing and reading material that uses these high-frequency units can help to promote both comprehension and fluency in language learning. Indeed, the importance of formulaic language has increasingly been recognized as fundamental to language knowledge and use, as evidence emerges to suggest that, while speakers may have explicit knowledge of some rules and patterns in language, they typically make use of a vast store of formulaic units that they use appropriately in a variety of situations. Hinkel (2012) is among the researchers and educators who argue that the bias against 'memorization' has prevented teachers and learners from taking advantage of a very effective way of expanding L2 users' repertoire of useful vocabulary, phrases, and larger units of language. We will return to this point in our discussion of fluency development.

Another factor that determines how input works for language acquisition is the salience of language features. Salience refers to how easy it is to notice a feature in the input. Noticing, in turn, affects the likelihood that learners will acquire that feature. For example, it is easier to notice *boy*, *two*, and *bird* in the sentence *The boy sees two birds* than it is to notice the –s that indicates the third person singular present tense verb (*see–s*) or the plural noun (*bird–s*) (Goldschneider & DeKeyser, 2001). In aural language input it is hard to hear grammatical markers such as function words and unstressed endings; in written input, the grammatical markers may also be overlooked while the focus is on the content words such as nouns and verbs.

Listeners and readers, including second language learners, tend to focus on the elements whose meaning is clearest and most important. Thus, in the example above, '*boy*' and '*bird*' are easier to notice, interpret, and learn than the grammatical markers. Indeed, function words such as *the* and grammatical endings such as the –*s* in *sees* may be redundant if we can get the information we need from the main words, prior knowledge, or an illustration (VanPatten, 1990). In CBLT classes, where so much attention is focused on meaning, students may acquire these redundant features very slowly or not at all.

Another factor that contributes to learners' ability to notice and learn language features is their position in the sentences or texts they hear (and read). Psychologists refer to this as 'primacy' and 'recency' effects, and these effects represent a consistent findings about how we process information. Numerous experiments have shown that it is easier to notice and remember the elements at the beginning and end of a string of words than it is to notice those in the middle. Research on language processing by Pienemann (1999) and his colleagues has shown how this can affect the way learners learn the word order of a second language. For example, learners of English are quick to notice the question words (*who*, *what*, *when*, etc.) that typically come at the beginning of a question. They learn to use these words in their correct position long before they learn to reverse the subject and auxiliary verb that come in the middle. A common and persistent error among English language learners is a question such as *When we're going to get our papers back?* In order to learn the non-salient features that are tucked away inside a string of words, students need guidance from instruction that places the focus on the language itself (Lightbown & Spada, 2013).

Recency and primacy effects are also relevant to the comprehension and recall of content, because information that is in the middle of a sentence is more difficult to notice and to process. As we have seen, comprehension can often be achieved by reliance on the main words, contextual cues, and background knowledge. For example, if learners hear (or read) *The soldiers were attacked by the townspeople* and they see an illustration of the event, they may pay no attention to the function words, verb forms, or word order because all they really need to know is in the picture. However, if they encounter the same sentence in the absence of an illustration, they may assume that the soldiers are the aggressors—partly because of expectations shaped by background knowledge, but also because of the strong tendency in English for the first noun in a sentence to be the subject (or the 'actor') and the noun following the main verb to be the object of the action. To get the correct meaning, they have to pay attention to the non-salient grammatical elements in the middle of the sentence—*were attacked by*. Thus, even comprehension can be affected if learners fail to take account of specific language features. In CBLT classrooms, students need guidance in understanding how these elements change meaning. Teachers can also help students by using techniques that focus attention on information that is buried in long paragraphs or texts, as well as the language features that are in the middle of sentences.

In summary, there is good evidence that comprehensible input is the essential starting point for second language acquisition, and there are many pedagogical techniques for helping students understand more of what they hear or read. However, it cannot be assumed that if learners grasp the general meaning of what they hear and read, language learning will take care of itself. Language development based on comprehensible input has limits—limits on which language features will be acquired, limits on learners' ability to use the language to express their own meanings, and limits on the continuing development of the language once basic communicative competence has been reached.

Very young children can acquire language primarily through incidental processes. For them, with sufficient time and opportunities to interact with language users, the new language may eventually be acquired. However, older children and adolescents typically have less time for these incidental learning mechanisms to work. Fortunately, they are also able to use more intentional learning processes, including the ability to analyze language. Indeed, classroom research suggests that they may depend on the skills they have acquired through their previous schooling and their cognitive maturity to keep their language acquisition moving forward, especially in a classroom setting where communicative interaction is emphasized (Muñoz, 2007b).

Helping students in CBLT learn content by making input comprehensible is of paramount importance. However, to ensure that they also continue to develop their L2 language proficiency, comprehensible input is not enough. We turn now to questions of how speaking and writing also affect the language acquisition process.

Comprehensible Output

In addition to recognizing the essential contributions of comprehensible input to language acquisition, researchers point to the value of producing meaningful language. Swain (2005) referred to this in her **comprehensible output hypothesis**, and many studies have explored the importance of speaking and writing—not as the result of language acquisition but as a process in the acquisition itself.

Swain's original formulation of this concept emphasized the fact that in comprehending language input, learners could often overlook specific linguistic features. As we saw in the discussion of comprehensible input, learners tend to focus on the main words to get the meaning. Indeed, with the help of a supportive context, much of language may be redundant, and if our only goal is comprehension, it is very efficient to focus only on the main words. Swain argued that learners are led to pay attention to the language itself when they must produce language for others to comprehend. In trying to produce language, learners discover what they do not know, and this discovery pushes their development forward.

Another way that speaking and writing promote language development is in eliciting a response from interlocutors (conversational partners) or readers. To a certain extent, this confirms Krashen's view that the value of output is that it reveals the level of language that learners can manage and elicits appropriate comprehensible input from interlocutors. That is, if learners show that their language ability is not adequate for an interaction or task, interlocutors may modify the language they use or the way they speak, for example, by speaking more slowly, repeating, or paraphrasing what they have said (Long, 1996).

In addition to modifying their own language to help learners achieve comprehension, interlocutors may help learners shape their output by providing **scaffolding**. Often discussed within the context of Vygotsky's Zone of Proximal Development, scaffolding refers to the kind of help that interlocutors can provide to learners who are encountering challenges in saying what they mean to say (Gibbons, 2002). By scaffolding, the interlocutor provides supportive language on which the learner can build, leading to the production of a clearer or more accurate or appropriate utterance that the learner may internalize so that it becomes a part of his or her own language knowledge.

Effective teachers use a variety of scaffolding techniques that allow learners with different proficiency levels to participate and learn in classroom interaction (Fortune, 2004). Gibbons (2009) emphasizes the importance of ensuring that students experience both 'high challenge' and 'high support' in the classroom. That is, students need to be challenged to do things that they can do only with support so that they can move their learning forward. In those experiences, which Gibbons calls the 'challenge zone', learners expand their knowledge and skill in ways that permit them to perform other tasks independently or in interaction with peers.

It is not only in interacting with teachers or other proficient speakers that learners benefit from producing language. They can also provide support for each other when they are engaged in group- or pair-work exchanges. Later in this chapter, and in Chapters 3 and 4, we will return to the important topic of how learners can support each other in learning both the academic content and the new language during cooperative and collaborative interaction.

Another kind of response that learners may elicit when they produce speech or writing in the new language is corrective feedback—information from others about gaps or errors in what has been said or written. We will return to this topic later in this chapter when we discuss the effectiveness within CBLT of instruction that focuses on language itself.

The Role of L1 in L2 Learning

There are three major questions with regard to the role of L1 in L2 learning. The first, which was touched on in Chapter 1 and in this chapter in the discussion of time on task, is whether students benefit from instruction that maximizes their exposure to L2 by limiting time spent in L1. The important conclusion of research on that question is that support for the development of literacy in students' L1 can result not only in the obvious advantage of additive bilingualism but also in greater proficiency in the L2 (Genesee et al., 2008). Furthermore, students benefit from knowing that their L1, which is an essential part of their identity, is respected by the educational community, even in situations where it is not possible for them to receive instruction through that language (Cummins & Early, 2011).

A second question concerns the influence of the L1 on the L2 during the acquisition process. That is, do students make errors or experience difficulty learning L2 because they try to use the patterns that they have learned in L1? Research on this question confirms that students' L1 does influence their perception of patterns in the L2 (Ringbom & Jarvis, 2009). In this, students are using prior knowledge to make sense of new knowledge—a learning strategy that is both inevitable and potentially useful (Ellis, 2009). There was a time when L2 educators thought that interference from the L1 was an impediment to L2 learning. Newer understanding of language acquisition and of the way the mind processes language suggests that trying to exclude the L1 from the learner's mind by excluding it from classroom language is neither necessary nor desirable (Cook, 2008).

The third question is whether the L1 should be used in the L2 classroom. If the answer to this question is affirmative, then we must also ask who should use the L1, how often, in what circumstances, and for what purposes. In foreign language learning situations, where students' only contact with the L2 is in the classroom and where total exposure to the language is measured in minutes per day, it may indeed be best to maximize exposure to the new language so that students will be motivated to focus on learning the new language rather than depending on the L1. Even here, however, L1 can facilitate learning when it is used for specific pedagogical purposes. In second language settings, however, there may be benefits in encouraging students to use their L1 as they think through a problem or to formulate a question about content or language (Antón & Di Camilla, 1998; Cook, 2001).

In classes where most or all of the language learners have the same L1 and where that language is also known by the teacher, there are strongly differing views about whether the L1 should be used at all and if so for what purposes. Some argue that helping students to identify the similarities and differences between their L1 and L2 can be an effective teaching strategy, as seen, for example in Spotlight Study 2.2.

Spotlight Study 2.2

In a series of descriptive and experimental studies, White (1998, 2008) has studied the **developmental sequence** in the acquisition of possessive determiners 'his' and 'her' by speakers of French. The acquisition of these forms is strongly influenced by the students' L1. In French, the gender of the possessive determiner is tied to the grammatical gender of the object possessed; in English, the gender of the determiner matches the natural gender of the possessor. For example, 'his father' and 'his mother' are translated as *son père* and *sa mère* respectively. French speakers learning English have difficulty internalizing this pattern.

White's research has included numerous pedagogical interventions designed to help young French speakers learn the English pattern. The students in several studies were 11- and 12-year olds in French-language schools in Quebec, in intensive ESL programs. These programs allowed students to spend more hours learning English than was typical for Quebec students. These were not CBLT classes. However, the instruction was based on a very strong commitment to communicative language teaching, and the teachers emphasized meaning-focused activities including group and project work almost exclusively (Lightbown & Spada, 1994).

White's (1998) first study involved increasing the frequency and the salience of the English forms in a variety of meaning-focused activities and emphasized comprehensible input rather than output activities. This approach did lead to some progress in students' passage through the developmental sequence, but errors persisted, especially when the object possessed was a noun referring to a family member with very marked natural gender (mother, father, etc.). That is, students might say 'his table' and 'her book', but they would also say, incorrectly, 'the boy is hugging her mother'.

In later studies, White increased the explicitness of the interventions. For example, students were taught a rule of thumb that directed them to 'Ask yourself whose it is' in choosing the correct form. In other activities, students learned to illustrate the direction of the agreement between the determiner and noun by drawing an arrow from the possessor to the determiner (for English) or from the possessed object to the determiner (for French). White found that this instruction, including explicit attention to the difference between English and French, led to more substantial gains than the activities that had simply increased opportunities for students to hear, read, and understand material containing large numbers of possessive determiners. ■

White's research was carried out in classes where students shared the same L1. In classes where minority-language students come from diverse backgrounds and speak different languages that their L2 teacher does not know, the issue might be considered moot. Even in this situation, however, some researchers and educators have proposed ways of drawing on students' L1 knowledge to enhance their L2 acquisition. Fu (2009) used her extensive research with Chinese and Spanish L1 students in New York City schools to show how encouraging students to use L1 for planning and even writing a first draft can lead to more effective writing in English. She acknowledges that thinking and writing drafts in the L2 'will help ELLs write in more idiomatic English than translating, which tends to be contaminated with their native expressions.' She goes on to argue, however, that 'for ELL writers at the beginning and even intermediate stages, this practice constrains thinking capacity, limits expression, and frustrates them tremendously in their writing process' (p. 27).

Other educators have encouraged students to reflect on 'how you say it in your first language' and to share that information in metalinguistic discussions of challenging aspects of L2 grammar and organization. The cognitive benefits of metalinguistic reflection are joined by the affective benefits of recognizing students' L1 as an important source of knowledge. Finally, Cook (2001) reminds us that code switching is a natural part of language use by individuals who know more than one language, and banishing the L1 from the classroom entirely does not acknowledge that reality. In Chapters 3 and 4, we will see some examples of students using L1 when they are working in groups—not to avoid using the L2 but to enhance their learning experience.

Language for Academic and Social Purposes

In Chapter 1, we noted that the types of language needed for social interaction among peers and for academic tasks have some different characteristics. These different kinds of language proficiency have been described by a number of researchers in different ways, but Cummins' original shorthand labels are still useful. He gave the label **of Basic Interpersonal Communication Skills** (BICS) to the kind of social language that may be observed when students interact informally. He used the term **Cognitive Academic Language Proficiency** (CALP) to characterize the kind of ability that is needed when students are using language in tasks that are cognitively demanding and also require the use of a particular kind of language—academic vocabulary, academic sentence types, academic register, or interaction style. Cummins' original labels have been much discussed and Cummins himself has elaborated on the characteristics that are typical of each kind of language use. This elaboration is often presented in terms of the graphic shown in Figure 2.1.

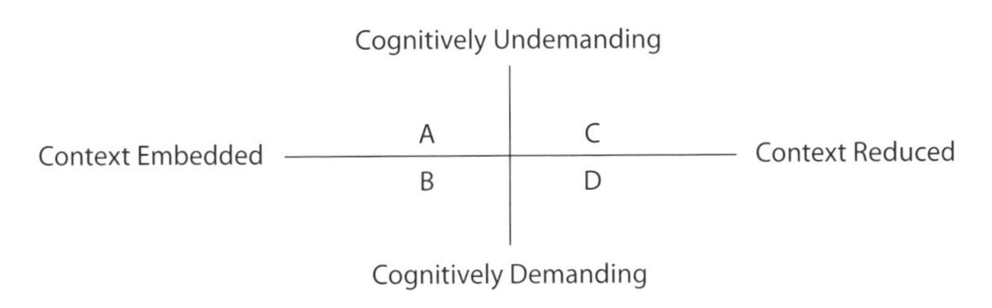

Figure 2.1 Cummins' framework: Contextual support and cognitive involvement in tasks and activities (2000, p. 68)

The degree of difficulty of using language in different situations is represented in the relationship between the dimensions of contextual support and cognitive demand. A language use event can be described in terms of its place in one of four quadrants. Events can occur in extreme corners of a quadrant or in a more moderate position, nearer the contrasting dimension. For example, the kind of language referred to by the BICS label is that which would occur in quadrant A. It is typical of informal conversation, in situations where the meaning is clear because of the circumstances in which the language is being used or the familiarity of the topic. A conversation with an unfamiliar person, talking about less familiar topics, might be seen as being slightly less context-embedded and more cognitively demanding, while still being positioned in quadrant A. A language event in quadrant C may more challenging but still manageable because, even though the context is less supportive, the language is familiar and the task is easy. In the classroom context, Cummins gives the example of drills or exercises, where the task is simple (cognitively undemanding) even if the associated meaning is not well supported by the situation (context reduced).

Quadrants B and D represent what Gibbons (2009) refers to as 'high challenge' situations that call for 'high support' from a teacher or other resource. The challenges are essential in pushing students forward to new learning, but they can also be frustrating if the right level of support is not available. Language use in quadrant B might include commentary about an ongoing science experiment. Meanings are made clear in part by the demonstrations, and although the content is challenging, it is reasonably easy to understand the meanings because of the relationship between the language and the contextual support provided by observable materials, actions, and outcomes. Quadrant D represents the most difficult learning situations. It might include activities such as reading an article about the Renaissance or listening to a lecture on the public health costs resulting from malaria. The content is cognitively demanding and lacks a supportive context.

In a classroom environment, teachers and students will use language in all four quadrants, of course. However, the goal of academic learning is to achieve the ability to work in quadrants B and D, where students try to learn new ideas, carried by language they cannot always use effectively, and with varying amounts of contextual support. Cummins observed, and other researchers have confirmed, that minority-language students who enter school without substantial prior education in their L1, may achieve BICS in one or two years, but it make take them five to seven—or even more—years to attain the CALP that is appropriate to their age and educational needs (Collier, 1987, 1989; Cummins, 1984, 2000; Thomas & Collier, 1997).

In some CBLT settings, the acquisition of BICS is more difficult than might be expected. Learning of this social register can be problematic when the relatively formal language of teachers and textbooks is the only model students are exposed to (Swain, 1981b). They do not encounter peers who are native or proficient speakers of the L2 with whom they can learn informal language or learn when to use certain pragmatic features that are appropriate for interaction with particular individuals who represent different levels of familiarity or status. Tarone & Swain (1995) drew attention to this concern, and other researchers have also investigated it in the context of immersion classes. For example, Lyster (1987) reported that Canadian French immersion students did not acquire certain social rules for using French outside the classroom, and research by Mougeon, Nadasdi, & Rehner (2010) confirmed that immersion students' speech often does not include language features that are typical of French as it is spoken by young native speakers in everyday usage. In Chapters 3 and 4 we will see examples of students' limited knowledge of social rules as well as some of the approaches that have been used to help overcome this limitation, including direct instruction on this aspect of language use and dual immersion programs that provide opportunities to interact with age peers.

More Insights from Cognitive Psychology

Cognitive psychologists study human learning in a wide variety of domains. In the following pages, we will look at two areas of this research that have particular relevance as background to the studies of language and content learning that we will explore further in Chapters 3 and 4. We will look first at **skill learning**, especially the role of practice in making sure that we get better at something we are trying to learn. Then we will look at several aspects of the study of memory, in particular, how our experiences in remembering what we have learned can improve the chances that we will be able to use the knowledge when we need it.

Skill Learning and Practice

Some theorists, most notably Krashen (1989), have argued that explicit instruction and metalinguistic information have little impact on language acquisition. They suggest that what is learned from explicit instruction serves only as a kind of monitor that allows a speaker or writer to correct a few things by applying rules after the message has been formulated using language knowledge that was acquired through comprehensible input. Others theorists argue, however, that explicit focus on language itself is an essential element of successful language development for learners beyond early childhood, especially for those who are learning a language in the limited time available at school (DeKeyser, 1998; Muñoz, 2006). Note, however, that explicit focus on language does not mean decontextualized drill and grammar exercises. Indeed, linking explicit focus on language to the language that is used in meaning-focused activities adds to its effectiveness.

Research on skill learning offers a way of conceptualizing the process of language acquisition. There are essentially three stages of skill learning. In the first stage, a learner becomes aware of new information—either by having had it explicitly taught or by the learner's own active noticing of it

(Schmidt, 1990). At this stage, the learner's knowledge can be described as *declarative knowledge*. Declarative knowledge is explicit and factual and can usually be stated in some way. Having this declarative knowledge does not ensure that the learner will apply it in new situations. In order for that to happen, the declarative knowledge must be developed through practice (DeKeyser, 2007). For example, having learned that the word 'salient' means 'easily noticed' the learner must encounter that word again in contexts where the meaning is reinforced. After sufficient practice, the declarative knowledge becomes *procedural knowledge*. At this point, the learner can easily understand the meaning of the word when it is comes up in new situations and even produce it appropriately.

The final stage in skill learning is automaticity or fluency, when the knowledge is accessed so rapidly and effortlessly that the language user no longer remembers not knowing it. At this stage, the knowledge is not only accessed easily but in fact cannot be suppressed (Segalowitz, 2010). Fluency is usually thought of in terms of production—fluent speaking or writing. However, fluency—**automatic** processing—is a goal for receptive language skills as well, including listening and reading. One famous illustration of automaticity in reading is the Stroop test. In this procedure, participants are shown words that are printed in different colors and instructed to name the color of the print as quickly as they can. That should be an easy task, and it is. However, when the participants see a word that is the name of a color that is different from the print color, their responses slow down perceptibly. That is, their performance on the easy task is impaired by the fact that they cannot *not* read and understand the word *red* written in green ink, even though they are trying to pay attention only to the print color. The ability to understand a large number of words effortlessly while reading is a significant contributor to successful reading comprehension.

The ultimate goal of language acquisition is to achieve automaticity, not only in processing words, but also in understanding and producing grammatical markers, formulaic phrases, word order, and other language features. The more language features learners can process automatically, the more attentional resources they have available to focus on the substance of what is being said as well as on new linguistic elements that are still to be learned. Ranta & Lyster (2007) discuss the application of skill learning to the language development of students in immersion education, emphasizing the importance of providing learners with feedback as they move from procedural knowledge to automaticity. They express concern that, without adequate feedback, learners will continue to practice incorrect language forms which will then become automatized (they use the term 'highly accessible') and thus very difficult to exclude from their **interlanguage**.

Ranta & Lyster propose what they call the 'awareness–practice–feedback' sequence that begins by making learners aware of the **target forms** they need to learn or to change, creating practice opportunities, and providing feedback over time to let the learner know if an attempt to use the language feature has been unsuccessful. Based on extensive research in CBLT contexts, they argue that for learners in settings such as Canadian French immersion classrooms, it is essential to do more than provide more comprehensible input. As they say, 'More input is not going to make a difference; learners need to be pushed when their focus is on academic content to use target forms which are in competition with highly accessible interlanguage forms' (2007, p. 153).

DeKeyser (1998, 2007) is among the psychologists who have emphasized the contributions of practice to language acquisition. He draws on a wealth of studies of human learning for evidence that repeated practice is essential for learning, but he also makes an important distinction between the kind of drill that was once common in language teaching and the kind of practice in using meaningful language that he sees as essential for successful language learning. DeKeyser argues that practice is specific. That is, we get better at what we practice, but we cannot count on practicing one kind of behavior to make us better at another. Thus, practicing language patterns in decontextualized drills or exercises will not prepare learners to use those language patterns in conversation. Practice in listening to language for the purpose of getting the general meaning may make us better at getting comprehensible input, but may not make us better at expressing our own meanings through speaking or writing. To get better at speaking and writing meaningful language, we need to practice exactly that—speaking and writing meaningful language. Furthermore, to return to the point made by Ranta & Lyster (2007), continuing to practice language forms that are incorrect or inappropriate may lead to automaticity in using those forms rather than the more accurate or appropriate ones that are associated with higher levels of proficiency.

Memory and Retrieval

Memory is an area of research in psychology that has probably generated more studies than any other. Two aspects of memory research are relevant to understanding language acquisition and content learning in CBLT: **encoding** (the internalization of knowledge) and **retrieval** (recognizing or recalling what we have learned). The term **working memory** (also referred to as short-term memory) refers to the processing of information that is in focus at a given moment and may or may not be encoded in long-term memory. For example, we use our working memory as we try to learn a phone number or a vocabulary list or to understand an explanation in a science textbook or a rule in a grammar book. Unless we have repeated opportunities to process the information that was briefly in focus in working memory, we are not likely to store it in long-term memory for retrieval at a later time.

One important fact about memory is that the capacity of working memory is limited while the capacity of long-term memory—though perhaps not infinite—is very large indeed. The analogy often offered is that working memory is like a computer's RAM, while long-term memory is like the computer's ROM. The computer's ROM capacity is very large, but only a limited amount of material can be processed in RAM. Like all analogies, this one has limitations, but it reflects the fact that we cannot 'think about' everything at once and that most of what we know is not in our active focus at any given time. The goal of learning is to be able to access elements of what is stored in long-term memory and to bring it into focus when you need it.

As we saw in the discussion of skill learning, research evidence shows that, in order to learn something, we must first perceive or notice it (Schmidt, 1990; 2001). We pay attention to it within the limitations of our working memory. When this occurs, we may or may not be aware of it or able to remember that we noticed it. Researchers have developed ways of showing how our cognitive processing may be at work on something that we are not aware of having noticed. One example is in priming studies, where language users, including second language learners, are more likely to use a particular word or language pattern if it has recently been used by their interlocutor in the conversation (Trofimovich & McDonough, 2011). Even if they cannot report having heard or noticed the word or pattern, it affects their behavior in measurable ways, in terms of both frequency and accuracy, showing that at some level, it has engaged their cognitive processing. Once again we see the importance of repeated exposure to material to be learned, sometimes in contexts of direct and focused instruction, sometimes in contexts where the material is present but not in focus.

One critical aspect of encoding new information is the connections that are made between that new information and other bits of information—old and new. When we encounter a new word, we may pay attention to the way it is spelled, what it means, how it sounds, what other words it reminds us of, the other words that occur with it. All of these things that we notice can become attached to the new word in networks of associations. Repeated encounters with the word give us new opportunities for adding new associations to that word's network. The more associations a word or phrase has, the more avenues we have for retrieving it later. This is related to the notion of depth of processing (Craik, 2002).

The research on retrieval of previously learned knowledge is complex and fascinating, and some of the findings are quite surprising. For example, psychologists have found that one of the best ways to learn something is to test yourself on it. That is, instead of reading a list or a paragraph over and over again, it is more effective to put it aside and try to remember it without looking at it, or to answer questions about it. This is referred to as 'effortful retrieval' or the 'test effect' (Bjork, 1994; Roediger & Karpicke, 2006). The test effect is often studied in combination with the spacing effect that we discussed above. When spaced practice is combined with the need to recall the material rather than have it presented again, long-term learning is enhanced. Thus, when we are learning a second language, we benefit from being placed in situations where we have to reach into our memory for something that we know but cannot yet access easily. The more often we do this, the greater the likelihood that eventually the knowledge will be accessible automatically.

Another important line of research on how we retrieve information is that which looks at **transfer-appropriate processing**. This research shows that remembering what we learn is easier when we are in a situation that is similar to the one in which we learned it in the first place or when using the kinds of cognitive processes that we used during learning. The notion of transfer-appropriate processing is based on the evidence that when we learn something, we internalize not only that which we intend to learn but also some aspects of the contextual features that were present and the cognitive processes we used when we learned it (Lightbown, 2008b).

Transfer-appropriate processing is related to the notion of the specificity of practice, discussed above. It helps to explain why, for example, students who have been taught grammar in a traditional grammar lesson, using explanations and decontextualized exercises, may do well on a grammar test that requires responses to exercises that are similar to those they practiced in their grammar lessons but fail to use the same grammatical forms during conversation. Learning the vocabulary and language patterns of a science experiment while carrying out an experiment is likely to result in a greater amount of transfer-appropriate knowledge than learning the same language in a separate lesson.

Taken together, the research on depth of processing and transfer-appropriate processing shows why it is so important for learners to encounter new language and new content in a variety of different activities, using a variety of different cognitive processes, practicing the material in different modalities (listening, speaking, reading, writing) and contexts, and linking it to previously acquired knowledge in as many ways as possible.

Corrective Feedback in Language Learning

In CBLT, teachers often say that their main concern is with making sure students learn the academic content. They recognize the importance of language learning but they often think that, given enough time and comprehensible input, students will gradually develop their knowledge of and ability to use the new language. As we have seen, they may also assume that the ability to use language for social interaction is evidence that students have reached age-appropriate L2 proficiency. Evidence from research in a variety of language learning settings, including a great variety of CBLT contexts, shows that students benefit from instructional guidance that focuses their attention on language itself.

One of the questions that is often asked about instruction that focuses on language is whether it should be provided in separate lessons or integrated into content-based lessons (Spada & Lightbown, 2008). We will see that the answer to that question is that both kinds of instruction are important for CBLT students, with the added observation that when language-focused instruction is separated from content classes, it should include focus on language features—vocabulary, grammar, style—that students will need while doing their academic work. Furthermore, during content-based lessons, the language features that were in focus in the language-focused instruction should be highlighted, and feedback on students' use of these features should be offered.

When learners produce spoken or written language in a CBLT context, a teacher or a peer may respond by continuing the conversation or reacting to the ideas that have been expressed. This could be seen as positive feedback, in the sense that the learner may see these responses as confirmation that what they said was understood. Alternatively, the interlocutor or reader might ask for clarification or show in some other way that the meaning was unclear or inappropriate. A peer would probably ask for clarification.

A teacher might request clarification or tell the learner more explicitly that something is incorrect. Either of these responses would be a kind of corrective feedback to the learner, indicating that something in the speech or written text did not quite accomplish its intended goals.

Teachers often express a reluctance to interrupt students to give feedback on a language error during a classroom activity where the focus is on academic content. They feel more comfortable offering feedback that focuses on what students are trying to communicate. In the CBLT context, this has been interpreted to mean, for example, that feedback on language form should be offered during a separate language-focused class, not during mathematics or science lessons. If they do provide feedback during content-focused lessons, they tend to provide implicit feedback, often in the form of a **recast** (a kind of 'echo' that retains the learner's meaning but in a correct form) rather than by offering a more explicit response to the *form* as opposed to the *content* of what students are saying.

Lyster & Ranta (1997) described different types of feedback on language form that they observed in French immersion classrooms. By far the most frequent type of feedback was the recast, and other researchers have found a similar high frequency of recasts in a variety of language teaching contexts. Lyster (2001) grouped feedback types into two main categories, those such as recasts that provide learners with the correct version of what they seemed to be trying to say and those that let the student know that there is a problem but then require the student to come up with a reformulation. The latter feedback types are referred to as 'prompts' and include requests for clarification, as well as more direct indicators (for example, a metalinguistic remark such as 'You should use the past tense') that the problem is with language form rather than the clarity or correctness of the student's apparent meaning.

It is evident that learners can self-correct only if they know what they should have said. However, there are two reasons to believe that prompts may be more effective in situations where students have some knowledge of the correct version but do not always use it. First, when teachers provide correct forms by offering a recast, students in CBLT classes may not recognize the feedback as being related to language form rather than content. An explicit correction makes that clear, but does not provide the other benefit of a prompt: the requirement that the student retrieve the correct form from memory. As we have seen, cognitive and educational psychology research has revealed the value of the so-called 'test effect' in which something is recalled from memory rather than being rehearsed through imitation or review in which the object of learning is present.

The recommendation to limit feedback to unobtrusive recasts during content classes may seem to be based on common sense and even on rules of politeness. The thinking seems to be that, when students are learning challenging new academic material, it would be wrong to distract them or interrupt them to draw attention to details of linguistic accuracy. It has been well established that cognitive resources, at least those that require the active engagement of working memory, are finite—learners cannot pay attention to everything at once. This is an important consideration and it is reasonable to worry that trying to pay attention to everything at once can lead to a failure to give adequate attention to anything! However, when we look at the research that has been done in classrooms, we will see how it is possible to respect this need to focus attention on a limited number of things while also taking account of another aspect of human learning that we have discussed—transfer-appropriate processing. That is, we will look at studies of how guiding students to pay attention to language during content lessons can help them improve their language proficiency.

If we want students to be able to use what they learn about language while they are engaged in meaning-focused academic content activities, it may be that the best time to provide feedback is while they are engaged in those activities. We will see, however, that there are important guidelines to help teachers decide what to focus on. For example, the research suggests that careful planning and focus on a small number of language features is more effective than responding to every error. One way of choosing what language features to focus on has been described in terms of **content-obligatory** and **content-compatible language** (Snow, Met, & Genesee, 1989). An example of content-obligatory language would be the vocabulary that is essential for the description and understanding of a science experiment. Content-compatible language would include the verb forms that are conventional in science reports.

Another reason that some educators have suggested that teachers provide only unobtrusive feedback is the concern that students do not want teachers to interrupt them to focus on language during content-based lessons. This view has been challenged in a number of studies of what students expect from teachers and how language and content learning are affected by feedback on language. Students in a variety of learning environments have expressed a preference for more feedback than their teachers are inclined to offer (Loewen et al., 2009; Schulz, 2001). In CBLT, far from being a 'settled' question, the matter of how and when to provide feedback continues to be a topic for debate and research.

Cooperative/Collaborative Learning

It has become a widely accepted pedagogical practice to have students of all ages work cooperatively in pairs or groups. Researchers and educators have found evidence that interaction between learners is an effective alternative to more traditional teacher-centered approaches, allowing students to become more actively engaged with the content and providing each other with opportunities to learn through dialogue (Slavin, 1994). Donato (2004) distinguishes between *interaction* and *collaboration* and shows how genuine collaboration makes unique contributions to language pedagogy.

McGroarty (1989) summarizes some of the benefits of cooperative/collaborative activities for language learners. First, she points out that in whole-class 'competitive' instruction, students who already speak the language well may dominate the interaction, leaving the language learners with little opportunity to engage in the academic discussions. She suggests that cooperative learning can be beneficial to CBLT students for both language and content learning. For language learning, cooperative activities engage students in a greater variety of language features and of language use, requiring both input and output and multiplying opportunities for students to use language meaningfully. For academic content learning, McGroarty notes that cooperative learning is beneficial because of the increased opportunities for more and different types of practice and greater engagement with the material as students take responsibility for aspects of their learning. She also sees cooperative learning as a positive environment for the development of social skills among learners, something that is difficult to develop in classrooms that are dominated by teacher-centered activities.

Some teachers worry that cooperative learning is not a good option for students who do not speak the classroom language well, especially if the students share the same L1. There is a concern that they will revert to their L1 rather than strengthening their L2 skills and that they will be unable to help each other resolve difficulties or provide feedback on errors. Research in a variety of CBLT contexts has shown that such concerns have some foundation. Nevertheless, when the tasks students engage in are well planned and organized according to the language abilities of the group members, they can succeed in developing both language (Swain & Lapkin, 2001) and content knowledge (Klingner & Vaughn, 2000).

Gibbons (2002, pp. 21–6) provides an excellent list of principles for teachers to keep in mind in order to ensure the best results in group-work:

- Clear and explicit instructions are provided.
- Talk is necessary for the task.
- There is a clear outcome for the group-work.
- The task is cognitively appropriate to the learners.
- The task is integrated with a broader curriculum topic.
- All children in the group are involved.
- Students have enough time to complete tasks.
- Students know how to work in groups.

None of these principles can be taken for granted, and there is no doubt that learning to plan and carry out effective group-work takes time and motivation—from both teachers and students (Oliver, Philp, & Mackey, 2008). However, the time and effort are well spent if the result is more opportunities for students to engage in meaningful language use, practicing what they have learned, increasing their self-confidence, and enhancing their motivation to keep trying. Minaya-Rowe & Calderón (2003) outline cooperative learning activities that are appropriate for school-age second language learners at every stage of language development—from beginning to advanced. We will look at some examples of students working together in primary and secondary classrooms in Chapters 3 and 4.

Vocabulary Learning

Children whose home language and school language are the same will know thousands of words on the first day they come to school. Thus, L2 children who are placed in mainstream classes start out with a huge vocabulary deficit. And, as Cummins (2002) and others have noted, an age-appropriate vocabulary is a 'moving target' because L1 students will continue to add hundreds of words to their vocabulary every year, and every year the vocabulary of academic content grows larger and more challenging. There is wide agreement that vocabulary is the key to comprehension, in speaking and in reading (Benjamin & Crow, 2010). Research by Nation (2001) and others shows that a limited vocabulary is the greatest impediment to successful reading comprehension—the most important tool for successful academic learning.

Research with L1 children shows that many thousands of words are learned without direct teaching (Nagy, Herman, & Anderson, 1985); and Krashen (1989) is well known for his view that 'we acquire vocabulary and spelling by reading.' The argument that vocabulary comes primarily from reading is based on the observation that, although words that are important for specific subject matter may be taught to L1 students as they study history ('treaty'), literature ('dénouement'), geography ('longitude'), or mathematics ('integer'), many more are learned incidentally through repeated exposure during reading.

Analyses of spoken and written language samples show that more than 80 percent of the words students encounter in English academic materials are likely to come either from the 2,000 most frequent words (Nation, 2001) or from the **academic word list** of 570 words that are common to a variety of academic subjects (Coxhead, 2000). This may suggest that once L2 learners have acquired some 2500 words, they should be able to read most texts. However, a text in which 20 percent of words are not known is very difficult to read with understanding, as you can see from Activity 2.1.

Activity 2.1

The paragraph below comes from an academic text that might be used in a teacher education program to provide background for teachers who are preparing to work with L2 or bilingual learners. You will probably find that, even when you know more than 80 percent of the words, you have difficulty making sense of the paragraph or guessing the meaning of the words you don't know. There are 82 running words in the text and 15 of them (18 percent) have been replaced by non-words. Because some of these non-words are repeated, this text may be easier to read than one in which 15 different words are unknown. Can you guess the meaning of the words that have been replaced by non-words in the text?

> It is important to clespeg working memory and fonwalger processing from Cummins' flapset of common underlying eropiensky. Cummins' flapset is clearly language dependent and vielepagonts in nature. In contrast, underlying cognitive bibesogti are thought to be fundamentally cognitive and nonlinguistic in nature and are part of one's innate lapebmesot—they are not learned. More netasally, Cummins' flapset of language for gleosich purposes is clearly an acquired eropiensky that is intimately culped to language topealk, in contrast with fonwalger processing and working memory.
>
> (Genesee et al., 2008, p. 67).

Note: You will find the original text at the end of this chapter.

Clearly this is a very great challenge. You can probably guess whether a word is a noun or a verb by looking at its place in the sentence, and 'netasally' contains a hint that it's an adverb. But to guess what the actual word is or even to guess its meaning, you would probably need to already have a pretty good idea of what the writers want you to learn from this text. In most school texts, we expect students to learn new information from what they read. What have you learned from this text?

Even when nearly all the words in a text are known, it can be difficult to learn new words by guessing their meaning while reading. Unknown words may appear in contexts that do not make their meaning clear. Beck, McKeown, & Kucan (2002) give the following example from a story students might read at the middle school level:

> Sandra had won the dance contest, and the audience's cheers brought her to the stage for an encore. 'Every step she takes is so perfect and graceful,' Ginny said grudgingly as she watched Sandra dance.
>
> (Beck et al., 2002, p. 4)

For a reader unfamiliar with the word *grudgingly*, the context seems to suggest that Ginny was full of admiration for Sandra. Even knowing all the other words in the paragraph would not help here. As Beck et al. point out, the immediate context is not only not helpful, it is misleading. Although the meaning might become clear in the larger context of the story, it might also lead the reader to be confused by Ginny's subsequent behavior if she is expected to show appreciation for Sandra's talent.

Thus, for a variety of reasons, it can be difficult to learn new words by guessing their meaning. Furthermore, researchers have shown that when learners encounter an unknown word in a text, they often manage to get the general idea without stopping to notice the word they don't know. Even if they do manage to figure out the meaning of the new word, they are not likely to remember it unless they have other reasons to pay attention to it. That is, without focused attention, they may 'understand' the word but not learn it (Hulstijn, Hollander, & Greidanus (1996).

Successful vocabulary learning will come from activities that ensure multiple opportunities to encounter words in a variety of contexts, using a variety of cognitive processes, in spaced practice over time (Zimmerman, 2009). Researchers have found that a word must usually be encountered many times before it becomes part of a learner's vocabulary. Some words may be learned after seven or eight encounters; others may not be learned until they have been seen dozens of times in a variety of contexts (Pellicer-Sánchez & Schmitt, 2010). The exact number of times is not fixed, and there are many factors that might make a word more or less meaningful and memorable. Nevertheless, we may assume that it is not the same number for the kind of learning that permits us to say, 'Yes, I think I've seen that word before' or 'Yes, I know that word quite well and I use it correctly in my own speaking and writing' (Nation, 2001).

Finally, we learn from research on learning vocabulary through reading that in order to substantially increase vocabulary size, one must read a great deal (Horst, 2005) and one must read a variety of text types (Gardner, 2004). In Chapter 3, we will look at research showing why not all reading material will provide students with opportunities to learn **academic vocabulary**.

In summary, we have seen that while guessing the meaning of a new word from context is an important skill, we have also seen that it is very difficult, it is not something that students will necessarily do successfully, and it may not result in actual word learning. Even though researchers have shown that, to guess the meaning of a word from its context, the reader must already know 95 to 98 percent of the other words in the text, the 'Sandra' text shows us that even when we know every word but one, the meaning of the unknown word may still be inaccessible without some other source of information.

A Framework for CBLT Pedagogy: Nation's Four Strands

In the final section of this chapter we turn to a pedagogical framework that is useful for conceptualizing the essential contexts for learning both language and content in CBLT. Nation (2007) has described language learning and teaching in terms of four strands. Descriptions of the four strands were developed in the context of Nation's research on vocabulary learning. However, the ideas are compatible with what research has shown about second and foreign language learning in general, not just vocabulary learning. Furthermore, because of the emphasis on meaning-focused activities, the four strands may be seen as helpful in understanding how CBLT can promote both content and language learning. **Nation's four strands** provide a way of organizing a lesson or a curriculum plan to include the range of contexts and activity types that learners need to ensure that their language development progresses as they continue to learn academic content appropriate to their age and their L2 proficiency.

The four strands are defined below. Three of the strands focus on meaning, while one focuses on the language itself. In CBLT settings, activities in the three meaning-focused strands can be seen as those in which students work to understand the academic content and have opportunities to use the language that is obligatory for or compatible with that content and which is at a level of difficulty that the students can manage. The fourth strand draws attention to language explicitly but does so in a way that prepares students for further language use and language learning in the meaning-focused content-based activities.

Meaning-Focused Input

Students listen and read for meaning. As with Krashen's comprehensible input hypothesis, the expectation is that students will be able, with a reasonable amount of effort, to understand what they hear or read. If this meaning-focused input contains only a limited number of new language features that can be understood within their context or with a brief dictionary check or question to a peer or teacher, students can acquire some new language features as they maintain a focus on the meaning. In a CBLT context, this strand could include activities such as reading a chapter in a high school history textbook, listening to a story while sitting in a circle in the kindergarten class, watching a video about climate change, or interacting with the teacher or other students in a discussion about how to multiply three numbers.

In order to ensure that students can focus on meaning during a particular task or activity, teachers may prepare students by getting them to anticipate what they will hear or read. Such preparation could include 'setting the stage' by introducing the topic to be covered, reminding them of what they already know about the topic, getting students to predict what they are going to learn, or providing some key vocabulary that they will need. As we saw in the 'washing clothes' experiment, such preparation can make a significant difference in the likelihood that information will be understood and remembered.

Meaning-Focused Output

Students speak or write for the purpose of conveying meaning. As suggested in Swain's comprehensible output hypothesis, students may encounter challenges in expressing themselves. In that case, they may need to look up words, ask a peer or teacher for assistance, or consult a classroom poster showing helpful vocabulary, language patterns, and formulas. As with meaning-focused input, the primary focus stays on meaning, but the need to produce language—whether orally or in writing—means that the student must pay attention to how the intended meaning is expressed.

Meaning-focused output may require some effortful retrieval of language items that the learner knows at some level but does not use frequently. In a CBLT context, this strand could include pair- and group-work in a cooperative learning activity, reporting on the observations of a science experiment, telling a story, doing a 'show-and-tell' activity for the class, writing to friend on a social media site, or writing a book report.

Fluency Development

Students understand and produce language that they already know but may not yet access automatically. In many contexts, this is the most neglected of the strands. Teachers and students may feel that once learners show that they are able to understand and express meaning, it is not appropriate for them to go over familiar material again. As we have seen in the discussion of skill learning, however, the final goal of learning is to be able to use language automatically, freeing attention for focus on meaning or on new language features. Furthermore, increasing fluency has motivational value, permitting learners to use language easily and confidently.

The term *fluency* is sometimes used in contrast to *accuracy*. That is not appropriate in the context of Nation's four strands definition of fluency. Activities in this strand place students in situations where they use familiar language and use it repeatedly so that it becomes easier and easier to access automatically. Nevertheless, the focus in this strand is on meaning. Activities should engage students in using language that is easy for them, but in contexts where there is a natural and reasonable expectation of multiple repetitions of this familiar language (Gatbonton & Segalowitz, 2005).

Within CBLT, fluency development could include activities such as practicing multiplication tables, carrying out a survey for a social studies class (asking several classmates the same questions), giving the daily weather report, performing a skit based on a story read in a language arts class, reading a simple story aloud to a younger student, silently reading fiction or nonfiction texts that are at an easy level for the student, playing guessing games or memory challenges that require the repetition of certain questions, listening to stories, or watching a familiar video. Songs, poems, and skits can also be effective in getting students to produce useful language units fluently. Activities in this strand can incorporate a focus on the formulaic units and frequent patterns that are appropriate within a particular context.

It is worth repeating that the fluency development strand does not call for decontextualized drill, where students repeat sentences over and over again outside a meaningful context, nor does it include language activities in which students find themselves needing words or language patterns that are not already familiar. Fluency development takes place through repetitive *meaningful* language use.

A final important point that may have become apparent from the above examples: fluency, in this context, does not refer exclusively to oral production. Rather, the goal is to develop fluency in all four of the traditional language skills—listening, speaking, reading, and writing. As we saw in the discussion of practice for skill learning, we become better at what we practice. Therefore, it is crucial that students have opportunities to practice both comprehension and production of language that they have begun to learn but have not yet automatized.

Language-Focused Learning

The fourth strand is language-focused learning. The emphasis in this strand seems clear from its name. Activities are designed for the purpose of drawing attention to features of the language itself. What may not be immediately clear from the name of the strand is the importance of ensuring that language-focused activities have a link to the language needed in the meaning-focused strands. As a number of researchers have observed, this connection between language-focused and meaning-focused activities has often been missing in CBLT instruction. In this strand, attention may be drawn to new language features or to accuracy in using previously learned ones.

The learners' age and previous educational experience will determine whether formal metalinguistic terminology is appropriate, but during these activities students need to know that they are looking *at* language, not *through it* to the meaning it represents. In classes where meaning-focused input and output activities are primarily oral, opportunities to see the language in written form and to manipulate the elements in a sentence or phrase can help students recognize the segments and patterns that are difficult to perceive in oral language. Explicit comparisons of L1 and L2 patterns are also appropriate in this strand.

The result of work in this strand may be immediate in the sense that learners find the answer to a question they have been asking themselves about how to say something. Or the activities may serve to increase the chances that, in subsequent meaning-focused activities, they will benefit from opportunities to practice using a language feature that was highlighted in the language-focused activities.

Activities in this strand might include a lesson on the verb forms that are needed for a science report, a dictation that includes patterns and vocabulary that occur in a social studies lesson, pronunciation practice, or fill-in-the-blank stories where the blanks are chosen to draw attention to particular language patterns. Learners may engage in language-focused activities under a teacher's guidance or they may work on their own, using reference materials or asking questions about the language.

Corrective feedback is also a part of the language-focused strand. Thus, language-focused learning may, at times, be integrated within meaning-focused activities. At other times, it is more appropriate to separate the language-focused and meaning-focused activities. This does not mean, however, that the language-focused learning is unrelated to those activities. It simply means that, for a specific period, there is no competition for the students' attention.

Finally, the language-focused strand also includes 'learning to learn' activities. This can include learning how to break down an unknown word into parts that may give a clue to meaning or learning to use reference books and dictionaries. It may also include the development of learning strategies that will improve students' ability to access and retain the content in meaning-focused lessons, whether in sheltered instruction or in the mainstream.

Weaving the Strands

Nation argues that all four strands are essential for language acquisition and are of equal importance and that students need to devote approximately equal time to each. The content of activities in each strand will change as learners advance in proficiency, but the principles remain the same: three-quarters of a learner's activities should be primarily meaning-focused, while one quarter of the activities should be focused on learning new aspects of the language or on more accurate and sophisticated use of those features that are already known. However, even that one quarter of time spent on language-focused activities is most effective if connections are made between what is learned there and the language that is needed for the meaning-focused activities.

It is apparent that some classroom activities primarily reflect one strand. For example, students get meaning-focused input when they listen to a teacher's explanation or read a textbook chapter and focus on understanding the academic content. Similarly, a student who is standing before the class in a show-and-tell activity is primarily engaged in meaning-focused output. Of course, this activity provides meaning-focused input for the other students. Many activities incorporate multiple strands. For example, working together to write a report on a science experiment, students will be producing meaning-focused output that constitutes meaning-focused input for other members of the group. It is likely that they will also engage in language-focused learning as they look for the right words or phrases to describe and explain their hypotheses, procedures, and findings. If they present their report to more than one group of fellow students, they may also be engaged in fluency development.

Like other pedagogical suggestions, Nation's four strands should be understood in the larger context of an instructional program. If CBLT students are in a foreign language context, it is likely that the classroom and its associated activities such as homework assignments will be the only source of learning in all four strands. On the other hand, minority-group students, who hear the language from their peers in mainstream classrooms and in the larger community may already have access to a significant amount of meaning-focused input and output. What they may need from the teacher is more opportunity for language-focused learning including 'learning to learn' strategies (Kinsella, 1997) and fluency development that will equip them with the language they need for getting help from peers and teachers. Whether in foreign language or second language contexts, the language-focused learning and fluency practice that will be most effective is that which is related to the students' uses of the language in content-based instruction.

In Chapters 3 and 4, we will look at research on language learning in various CBLT settings and we will have occasion to consider whether learners in these settings have access to all of the learning opportunities that are suggested by Nation's four strands.

Summary

Research by applied linguists, psycholinguists, cognitive psychologists, and educational psychologists provides a basis for understanding how some things we do in the classroom succeed in helping learners make progress in both language and content. The research reviewed in this chapter suggests that comprehensible input is the starting point for language acquisition. It also shows that learners who need to produce language that is comprehensible to others will make greater progress in language development. The research has shown that practice is essential and that, for the practice to have the greatest benefit, learners must have access to feedback that helps them know when they have succeeded and when their language still needs improvement. The research we review in Chapters 3 and 4 will draw on these findings and show how they explain some successes and failures in classroom learning of language and content.

Here is the original text for the '80 percent text' on page 63.

> It is important to distinguish working memory and phonological processing from Cummins' notion of common underlying proficiency. Cummins' notion is clearly language dependent and developmental in nature. In contrast, underlying cognitive abilities are thought to be fundamentally cognitive and nonlinguistic in nature and are part of one's innate endowment—they are not learned. More specifically, Cummins' notion of language for academic purposes is clearly an acquired proficiency that is intimately linked to language experience, in contrast with phonological processing and working memory.
>
> (Genesee et al., 2008, p. 67)

3 Classroom-Based Research on CBLT with Young Learners

Preview

In Chapter 2, we reviewed general issues from the research on learning, learning language, and using language to learn academic content. We have seen that learners can acquire a great deal of language while their attention is focused on meaning. However, when language features are rare or non-salient or when their meaning is redundant because a more frequent or salient language form carries the same meaning, learners may be exposed to the language for hundreds or even thousands of hours without ever realizing that what they are doing differs from what more proficient speakers do.

In this chapter we will relate the general research findings on learning content and language to real students and teachers in CBLT classrooms, from Pre-K to Grade 6. The focus will be on the kinds of pedagogical strategies teachers use to help young learners improve their language proficiency while also learning the content appropriate to their grade level.

Activity 3.1

Drawing on your own experience and that of other teachers, answer the following questions:

- Do you think young learners can benefit from feedback or instruction that focuses on language form?
- Do you think there is a difference between how students in Grades K–3 and 4–6 respond to a focus on language form during CBLT?
- Do you think there is a difference between the way teachers react to vocabulary errors and the way they react to errors of grammar or pronunciation? If so, what do you think those differences are and what do you think might lead to them?
- Do you think there is a difference between how ESL-trained teachers and content-trained teachers without ESL training attend to language form when they are teaching a content-based lesson?

Keep your answers to these questions in mind as you read about research on how CBLT teachers provide instruction and feedback on language and content for students in the Pre-K–Grade 6 age group.

What Do Students Need to Learn in Primary School?

It is commonly said that in early primary school, students learn to read, but in the later years, they must read to learn. For this reason, the development of literacy skills is usually given the highest priority for young learners. From pre-kindergarten to Grade 2, children who are being schooled in their L1 develop basic reading and literacy skills such as sound–letter correspondences, decoding and comprehension, sentence construction, and handwriting. At the same time, they are learning the social and cultural rules of going to school. Second language learners must do the same things, but they must also develop oral proficiency in a second language at the same time. In the years from Grade 3 to Grade 6, students must use their evolving literacy and cultural knowledge to acquire the academic and linguistic skills that prepare them for the secondary school.

Children who enter school as second language learners at the pre-kindergarten or kindergarten level benefit from many opportunities to follow their peers as they engage in a variety of tasks associated with learning what it means to go to school. In observing a kindergarten class in a dual-immersion school, DePalma (2010) found that language does not always play the role she had anticipated in these early school experiences.

> … children's interactions often did not require any language at all. Over and over, I witnessed children share classroom tasks and play together happily without saying much at all, and the activity unfolded perfectly well without the linguistic interactions so fundamental to the [dual immersion] model.
>
> (DePalma, 2010, p. 3)

Young children can give the impression that they understand the teacher's language by imitating the actions and words of others. As school routines become familiar, they will know when to line up at the door, sit on the 'reading rug', or take out their pencils. These opportunities to be engaged in classroom interaction even when their language is very limited provide comprehensible input that will allow them to make connections between the classroom activities and the language that occurs in these settings.

Tabors & Snow (1994) describe preschool classrooms in which second language learners who were not yet able to speak English used what the authors call 'spectating' and 'rehearsal' as strategies for participation and gradual access to the language. In spectating, children may remain silent while intently watching the faces and mouths of other children and adults who are speaking the new language. In rehearsal, children may repeat the words of another speaker, but they may do so in a whisper or even by simply mouthing what they have picked out in the language they have heard. Other research provides further examples of how young learners can benefit from opportunities to learn from their peers (for example, Wong-Fillmore, 1983).

Teachers may not always be aware of how children can take advantage of the language around them. In her study of kindergarten and Grade 1 English language learners from a variety of L1 backgrounds, Toohey (2000) observed that teachers often discouraged students from imitating others or from seeking help from their peers. These behaviors were seen as inappropriate in the school environment. What we know about early stages of language development suggests that, rather than prohibiting these behaviors, teachers might help students more by encouraging them in classroom activities where it is appropriate, while eventually leading students to understand when 'copying' and 'borrowing' are not allowed.

As students advance through the grades, the level of language proficiency that is required for success in performing academic tasks changes. More and more of the tasks they carry out make use of decontextualized language—language whose meaning cannot be guessed from illustrations or gestures. Students who seem to have been doing well in school start to experience difficulties. References to a 'fourth Grade slump' are often seen, and this decline is not limited to ELLs. Chall & Jacobs (2003) describe the pattern they observed in their research with students in Grades 4–7 whose reading ability had developed in an age-appropriate way through Grade 3, but then began to diverge from the 'normative population' of students from families with higher income:

> The first and strongest to slip was word meaning. The low-income children in our study—in Grades 4 through 7—had greatest difficulty defining more abstract, academic, literary, and less common words as compared with a normative population on the word meaning test. In Grade 4, the children were about a year behind grade norms. By Grade 7, they were more than two years behind norms. Next to decelerate were their scores on word recognition and spelling. Oral reading and silent reading comprehension began to decelerate later in Grades 6 and 7.
>
> (Chall & Jacobs, 2003, no page number)

Minority-language students who enter mainstream classes in Grade 3 or later are less able to pretend they understand, nor can they always count on help from contextual cues or an instructional program that meets their needs. Majority-language students in CLIL or immersion classes that are specially designed for second language learners may have the benefit of a program of instruction that is designed to take account of their status as language learners. In any case, as they progress through the grades, students are increasingly expected to learn cognitively complex material, presented in academic language. Their reading must move beyond simple decoding to an ability to interpret text. That includes understanding what is explicit in the text, but also understanding what is implied but not actually written. And academic language is not only the written language of textbooks or assignments, it is also the instructional language that is spoken by the teacher. Older second language learners who have had interrupted schooling or have not acquired literacy in their L1 must also meet the challenge of learning the social and cultural rules of being in a classroom at an age when this kind of knowledge has already been acquired by other students (Brinton, Sasser, & Winningham, 1992; Hamayan, 1994).

One issue that has been the source of controversy in CBLT for young learners is whether they should be taught to read first in L1 or L2. The basis for transitional bilingual education programs is the belief that learning to read first in the L1 gives learners several advantages: they build on existing vocabulary knowledge to enhance their comprehension of what they read; they know what words and phrases sound like, making it easier to learn sound–letter correspondences if they are learning an alphabetic language; having learned the principles of how reading and writing work in their own language allows for an easier transfer of skills to the L2.

Research with minority-language students often finds advantages for students who have acquired L1 literacy before they begin learning to read in the L2. Other studies have found that teaching students in their L1 and L2 at the same time is also more effective than teaching in the L2 only (Slavin & Cheung, 2005). Students in CLIL programs and the European Schools focus primarily on developing reading and writing ability in their L1 in the earliest years of schooling. L2 is introduced mainly in oral communicative activities until the later years of primary or even secondary school (Housen et al., 2011).

The idea that early literacy in L1 is a good foundation for L2 learning has been supported by research in a number of contexts (Dixon et al., 2012; Genesee et al., 2008), but much remains to be understood about how L1 and L2 reading affect each other, especially for students whose L1 does not use the same writing system or has very different structural patterns from those in the L2 (Oller & Jarmulowicz, 2009). In immersion programs for majority-language students, young readers have had success with literacy instruction that starts with L2 (Genesee, 1987). Researchers have found that, having been taught to read in their L2, students quickly transfer their skills to the L1 and need little direct instruction in L1 reading. What both the European and immersion programs have in common is that support for reading and writing ability in the L1, whether present at the beginning or introduced later, is considered a priority for students' education.

Spotlight Study 3.1 provides insight into the question of initial literacy training in L1 or L2.

Spotlight Study 3.1

As we saw in Chapter 1, dual immersion programs were developed in part to allow interaction among students from majority- and minority-language groups as they learn each other's language. In some US schools, the terms 'minority' and 'majority' language have taken on an interesting twist. For example, in some states, there is a growing number of schools where the majority of the population are of Hispanic background, but ethnic background and immigration status cannot be used to predict students' language proficiency. Children in these schools may speak Spanish at home or they may come from families where English is spoken most of the time. Dual immersion has proved to be an effective way of educating children from both groups.

Lindholm-Leary & Block (2010) followed groups of students from a Hispanic background who entered school as ELLs and their peers who were deemed to be English proficient (EP). Their study took into account differences in socioeconomic background, especially the level of parents' education. They analyzed learners' progress over several years, comparing outcomes for students in dual immersion with others in mainstream instruction. It is noteworthy that the dual immersion programs in the study were similar to the Canadian early immersion models. That is, 90 percent of classroom instruction in the early school years was in the minority language, Spanish, with English language arts introduced only in Grade 3, and students received their first literacy training in Spanish. Students in mainstream classes, in contrast, received all their instruction in English.

By the end of elementary school, measures of both English and mathematics ability (assessed in English) showed overall better performance for students in the dual immersion programs. This was true both for students who had started school as EP and those classified as ELL. Parents' education could be seen as a contributor to students' success in all programs, but dual immersion programs were more effective than mainstream programs for ELLs whose parents had lower levels of education. In addition, of course, students in dual immersion instruction had acquired considerable proficiency in Spanish, in terms of literacy and performance on mathematics tests. Thus, both groups of dual immersion students showed that they were on track for developing additive bilingualism and its associated cognitive and social benefits.

Spotlight Study 3.1 is one of many studies that have found benefits for the dual immersion approach. In light of the controversy about the language in which students should learn to read, the finding that all students—whether ELL or EP—benefited from literacy instruction in Spanish is particularly important. One possible explanation for the benefit of early Spanish literacy training is that Spanish spelling is almost perfectly regular. In contrast, learning the correspondences between spelling and pronunciation of words in English is very challenging. It may be that having learned to read first in Spanish, students can more easily transfer their knowledge to the more complex sound–letter systems of English. When students learn to read in languages that have very different writing systems or structural properties, specific language transfer is not possible. Even so, general advantages of bilingual literacy are reported (Lindholm-Leary, 2011; Oller & Jarmulowicz, 2009).

Turnbull, Hart, & Lapkin (2003) investigated the academic and linguistic performance of Grade 3 and Grade 6 students in French immersion programs in Ontario, Canada, where as we have seen, students learn to read first in French, their L2. The researchers started from an earlier finding (Turnbull, Lapkin, & Hart, 2001) that students' performance on academic measures was typically below that of their English-educated peers in Grade 3 but closer to their peers—and often superior to them—in Grade 6. They noted two possible interpretations of this finding. First, the observed 'lag' could be due to the time it takes for second language learners to achieve sufficient L2 proficiency to enable them to master the academic content appropriate to their age level. This would be consistent with the observation, made by Collier (1989), Cummins (1984), and others, that students need five or more years to achieve academic language ability that is age-appropriate. A second possible interpretation of the finding is that it reflects a selection effect. That is, students who were experiencing difficulty might have chosen to leave the program, leaving only more academically gifted students in the immersion classes at Grade 6. Turnbull, Hart, and Lapkin found that neither time nor selection provided an adequate explanation, but they urged further study of how Grade 6 students were able to overcome the original lag in performance.

Clearly, minority-language students do not have the option of dropping out of their programs at this age, and the research by Chall and many others suggests that for minority-language students, as well as native speakers of English from low-income family backgrounds, performance on reading and other academic skills begins to decline, relative to more advantaged classmates, at about Grade 4. As the gap between their language and literacy abilities and those of their majority-language peers grows, the risks of academic failure also increase. The importance of ensuring that ELLs develop strong literacy abilities can hardly be overstated.

Learning the Content in CBLT

From the beginning, research reports on immersion programs in Canada showed that, for a few years, children had some lags in their English reading and academic content knowledge measured in English. However, these lags were quickly overcome once they had begun to have a few hours of English instruction each week, starting in about Grade 3. Meanwhile, they developed high levels of comprehension in French and kept up with age-appropriate academic content (Lambert & Tucker, 1972).

In Chapter 2 we reviewed the role of comprehensible input as the starting point for language acquisition. Comprehensible input is also the first requirement for learning academic content. It is true that some school subjects allow students to learn partly from observation and experience, but all academic learning includes the need to understand and eventually to produce the language that carries that content. Thus, in learning science, history, or even mathematics, students have to be able to understand and remember what they hear and read. This fact is at the heart of sheltered instruction, as suggested by the title of Echevarria, Vogt, & Short's (2012) book *Making content comprehensible for English language learners*. How can classroom instruction be designed so that students with limited language skills can understand subject matter that is appropriate for their age? There are two broad approaches that might be adopted: simplify the material or support students' interaction with the material.

Using simplified material might entail using texts or activities that are designed for younger L1 students or that are specially for L2 learners. The simplification may be reflected in a lower density of vocabulary, greater use of illustrations, or shorter, less complex sentence types. Such an approach has benefits for learners who are just beginning to learn the L2. Special, simplified materials can be motivating because students experience the success of understanding texts—oral and written—in the new language. And as we saw in the discussion of vocabulary learning in Chapter 2, reading texts that are beyond a student's proficiency can be frustrating and counter-productive. On the other hand, reading simplified texts that contain only a few new words provides meaning-focused input that allows students not only to understand what they read but also to learn new words and language patterns.

Simplified materials may also be useful in the mainstream classroom because they allow students with lower language proficiency to work independently on material that is within their grasp. Graded readers, for example, give language learners access to a wealth of content in books that are comprehensible to readers with very basic vocabulary knowledge and those with more advanced language knowledge. Publishers have responded to the need for such material by producing thousands of books, both fiction and non-fiction, for example, the *Oxford Bookworms* and *Read and Discover* series. Students at almost any proficiency level can find books that allow them to read independently and successfully. Such materials, in terms of Nation's four strands, provide opportunities for additional meaning-based input and for developing reading fluency. When these materials are used to supplement regular instruction, they can enhance both language and content learning.

The use of simplified materials has its limits, however, and the exclusive use of such material would slow students' progress in learning the age-appropriate content that is their goal. In immersion or CLIL classes, students need to have access to content that is appropriate for their grade level to avoid gaps in the knowledge they need for examinations that are often administered in their L1. In mainstream classrooms, using different material from that which other students are using can leave ELL students isolated and deprive them of opportunities to learn from the regular classroom instruction and from interaction with other students who are more proficient in the language. In addition, using simplified materials limits the content available for learning. For example, if they are using science materials that do not contain the content and the academic language that are appropriate for their age level, they will not be prepared to continue with their classmates to the next level in the science curriculum or meet the academic standards that are required for higher education (Kinsella, 1997; Wong Fillmore, 2010).

Thus, the use of special simplified materials may make some content comprehensible and provide an entry point for some L2 learners. However, teachers need to use other ways of giving students access to the content that is appropriate for their age and grade level. What are some of the pedagogical practices that teachers of students in elementary schools can use to make the regular content comprehensible? Classroom Snapshot 3.1 provides one example from a Grade 3 class.

Classroom Snapshot 3.1

The teacher whose lesson is described in this transcript is teaching mathematics in Spanish to Grade 3 students in a dual immersion program. You may recognize her as the teacher you first met in Classroom Snapshot 1.2, and you may recall that her students' Spanish proficiency varied greatly.

Students were seated at tables of four or five students. After a brief review of simple multiplication that had been the topic of previous classes, the teacher told the students that they were going to learn something new: the associative property of multiplication, that is, the fact that, when multiplying three or more numbers, the result does not change if the order of the numbers changes (for example, $2 \times 3 \times 6 = 6 \times 2 \times 3$). She then taught the lesson, and I observed the following pedagogical behaviors. In this lesson, the teacher:

- drew on students' prior knowledge by having them practice multiplying familiar pairs of numbers
- put examples on the board and discussed them with the whole class
- used technical mathematical language
- had students do examples in their workbooks
- encouraged students to discuss their work and help others seated at the same table if help was needed
- replied in Spanish if students spoke English and encouraged them to repeat the question in Spanish
- had groups of students come to the board and explain to others how they had solved a problem
- allowed students to get it wrong and then engaged the whole class in discovering why they had run into difficulty
- had students hold cards with numbers and multiplication signs, changing position as she asked the class whether the result was still the same
- asked students to explain some part of the procedure and always gave them plenty of time to answer, often inviting them to 'tell me more'
- asked students to speak loud enough for others to hear, ensuring that the conversation included the whole class, not just one student and the teacher
- asked the students what they had learned, eliciting both the technical term (the associative property of multiplication) and allowing several students to define the concept in informal language
- assigned some more examples for homework.

As soon as students had put their mathematics books away, the teacher called them to sit on the carpet, where she started a new science unit on plants, beginning by asking students to talk about what they already knew about the topic and using that information to develop some vocabulary graphics on a flip chart. No time was lost in moving between the mathematics and science lessons. One had the impression that, for this teacher, every classroom minute was precious.

People who are new at public speaking are often given the following advice: tell them what you're going to say; say it; then tell them what you said. It's excellent advice for a public speaker who wants to make sure that the audience understands and remembers their presentation. It is also good advice for CBLT teachers. However, in the classroom, we would want to add another element: get the audience to tell you what they have understood. The teacher in Classroom Snapshot 3.1 used all these elements to increase learning opportunities for content and language learning. This teacher's lesson allowed the successful participation of all students, including some whose Spanish language proficiency was considerably less advanced than others'.

It is noteworthy that in this dual immersion program, the paired English and Spanish teachers coordinate their lessons. Thus, having spent a week learning mathematics in Spanish, students will spend a week learning mathematics in English, but they will progress to the next lesson or textbook chapter rather than repeating what they have already done in the other language. In this way, students review content learned in one language, but they are expected to move forward by learning new material in each language. The teachers are bilingual, and this allows them to understand students when they use either language. However, they themselves almost always speak the language of instruction to all students during class time.

Group-Work in Content Learning

In the lesson from which Classroom Snapshots 1.2 and 3.1 were taken, students did do some work together at their tables, but this particular lesson (though by no means every lesson taught by this teacher) was primarily teacher-centered. What about other classroom interaction patterns? To what extent can students who are language learners benefit from working with other students, both those who are also learners and others whose language proficiency is more advanced?

McGroarty (1989) discusses cooperative learning in the context of content-area L2 instruction. She mentions a number of benefits of this approach to pedagogy, including the following:

- cooperative learning as exemplified in small group-work provides frequent opportunity for natural L2 practice and negotiation of meaning through talk.
- cooperative learning can help students draw on primary language [L1] resources as they develop second language skills.

- cooperative learning approaches encourage students to take an active role in acquisition of knowledge and language skills and to encourage each other as they work on problems of mutual interest.

(McGroarty, 1989 pp. 61–7)

Keeping McGroarty's 'benefits' in mind, look at Spotlight Study 3.2, which gives some insight into how some groups of young students with different levels of L2 proficiency can succeed in cooperative group-work.

Spotlight Study 3.2

Klingner & Vaughn (2000) studied cooperative learning in a Grade 5 class where English was the language of instruction. Nearly all the students spoke either Spanish or both Spanish and English at home. Some teachers might doubt the possibility of doing effective group-work in this environment. Citing work on cooperative learning by other educators, the researchers emphasize the importance of preparing not only the students but also the teachers to ensure that group-work will be effective. For this study, they trained the teacher, who in turn trained the students in the use of Collaborative Strategic Reading (CSR). Working in groups, students helped each other to understand a text from a science and health lesson. Their interaction was structured by four reading strategies, which Klingner & Vaughn describe in the following way:

1 *Preview:* Prior to reading, students recall what they already know about the topic and predict what the passage might be about.
2 *Click and clunk:* During reading, students monitor comprehension by identifying clunks, or difficult words and concepts in the passage, and using fix-up strategies (for example, looking for clues to meaning in surrounding sentences) when the text does not make sense.
3 *Get the gist:* During reading, students restate the most important idea in a paragraph or section.
4 *Wrap-up:* After reading, students summarize what has been learned and generate questions that a teacher might ask on a test.

(Klingner & Vaughn, 2000, p. 75)

Klingner and Vaughn recorded the students working in groups of six or seven. In keeping with cooperative learning principles, all students in each group had specific individual roles and responsibilities. In rotation, students served, for example, as the 'leader, clunk expert, announcer, encourager, or timekeeper' (p. 78) . As you read the transcript below, keep the following questions in mind:

- Can you guess, from the following short excerpt, what role each student is playing—leader, clunk expert, announcer, encourager, or timekeeper?

- How would you characterize this exchange in terms of the four strategies in the CSR listed above?
- Which students seem to have stronger English language skills? Which ones are less proficient? What gives you this impression?

Give examples of how the students' interaction represents McGroarty's proposed 'benefits' mentioned above.

Diana: Click and clunk?
Pablo: Calcium.
Greg: Try to read sentences in the back and in the front to try to get a clue. Think if you see any sentences in the back or in the front that can help you. Did you get anything?
Pablo: No.
Greg: OK, now I do, I get something. It is a tiny crystal-like mineral. Do you know what a mineral is?
Pablo: Yeah.
Greg: What is it?
Pablo: It's like a kind of vitamin.
Greg: OK, calcium is a type of element that there is in the bones. And, the bones need that. Calcium helps the bones in order to make them strong. Do you now understand what calcium is?
Pablo: Yes.
Greg: What is it again, one more time?
Pablo: It is a type of element that helps the bones grow.
Greg: OK, good.

(Klingner & Vaughn, 2000, p. 78)

What is most striking about this example is how focused students appear to be on their task. From this excerpt, we can conclude that they have been well prepared to do the work they need to do as a group.

Diana seems to be the leader. She has only one line in this exchange, but it is she who sets the agenda for the subsequent discussion. We can't tell much about Diana's English, but it is interesting to imagine that she might be able to play her role as leader here even with quite limited English proficiency, as long as she is well prepared for the task and has a clear idea of her responsibility to keep the activity moving.

Greg appears to be the 'clunk expert' but he also takes the role of encourager as he leads Pablo to discover what he already understands and makes sure that Pablo is able to produce a plausible definition of the word he has asked about.

We see the students engage in the 'click and clunk' discussion and we see an example of the 'wrap up' as Greg asks Pablo to answer a question about the role of calcium. In this short excerpt, it is clear that Greg's English is considerably stronger than Pablo's. He produces long sentences, uses the language creatively and is able to say the same thing in different ways as he seeks to help Pablo understand. Greg's final turn in this transcript is particularly impressive as he asks Pablo to state, once again, what he has learned, using a full definitional sentence. Greg appears to be using the CSR strategy of asking a question that 'a teacher might ask on a test.' It allows Pablo to practice what he needs to be able to do at a later time.

On the surface, this exchange is all about helping Pablo, and we might conclude that it is he who benefits most from this brief event. However, that would overlook the possibility that Diana has learned from the opportunity to hear Greg's explanation and that Greg also benefits from his practice in explaining. It is often said that the best way to learn something is to teach it to someone else. Greg may be providing an example of that.

Overall, Klingner and Vaughn found that students were capable of working effectively in groups and of helping each other. They stayed on task and used their time well. Their knowledge of the target vocabulary representing both language and content goals was measured on a pre-test and a post-test. All students showed some vocabulary growth, and most students showed substantial progress in learning the vocabulary. Interestingly, 'high achieving' students made the greatest gains, reinforcing the observation that working with less proficient students was also beneficial for their learning. ■

Spotlight Study 3.2 shows how the success of group-work depends crucially on ensuring that students are well prepared for the task and this in turn depends on the teacher's understanding of the goals and procedures of this learning approach.

Both the teacher-centered lesson in Classroom Snapshot 3.1 and the cooperative learning activity in Spotlight Study 3.2 show how learners in CBLT classes can manage age-appropriate academic content.

Learning the Language in CBLT

As we saw in Chapter 2, L2 learning begins when students have access to comprehensible input. As you read Classroom Snapshot 3.2, think about what you might say to the teacher. You may find that the young learners who are just beginning to receive instruction through their second language seem to have a better idea of what they need than their new teacher does!

Classroom Snapshot 3.2

In a Grade 3 classroom in northern Quebec, Canada, a new teacher was worried about how best to teach her students. Their home language is Inuktitut and this was also the language of instruction for them in kindergarten through Grade 2. When they reached Grade 3, however, their instruction was to be almost entirely in English, with Inuktitut used only for brief 'cultural' lessons each week. When we visited the class, the students had been in Grade 3 for just a few weeks. The teacher was very concerned about the fact that students seemed to want to spend as much time as possible sitting on the rug in the story corner, listening to her read stories from picture books. She asked for advice, saying, 'I can't spend the whole day reading to them!'

(Based on field notes. For more about this research context, see Spada & Lightbown, 2002.)

Several kinds of information might have helped the young teacher in Classroom Snapshot 3.2 feel less frustrated about what her students wanted to do. First, it would have helped her to realize that, at the earliest stages of language acquisition, learners should be focused on getting comprehensible input. Listening to picture-book stories read and discussed by their teacher was one good way to do this. And we have seen that this early stage of language learning is often characterized by non-verbal interactions during which children learn by observing, listening, and seeking to understand the language in their environment (Tabors & Snow, 1994).

In this particular learning context, the tendency to learn by listening and observing may have been even stronger, due to cultural practices in the community. As Crago (1992) discovered through her research with Inuit families, children in this society are expected to learn by watching and listening to adults, gradually beginning to imitate what they see adults doing. They are expected to be quiet and to speak only when spoken to. The kind of behavior that the new teacher expected—speaking out and raising a hand to signal the desire to talk—would have been considered inappropriate by their parents. Indeed, Crago describes an exchange between a parent and a teacher in which the teacher comments positively on a student's eagerness to participate and gets an apology from the parent! The assumption that young children must be talking to show that they are learning has also been questioned by Wong Fillmore (1983) who found that depending on the overall classroom dynamic, it may be the quiet students whose language development proceeds most successfully in the early school years.

For a number of years, most research with majority-group students in immersion programs focused on their academic performance and the retention and development of their L1. As we have seen, researchers found that students who started French immersion in kindergarten did well on academic subject matter and, after a brief lag, on academic performance—including reading—in English, their L1. Once teachers and parents were convinced that French immersion students would not lose their L1 or fall behind in academic work, more attention was paid to their success in learning French. From the very beginning of the experiment, Lambert & Tucker (1972) had taken account of students' French language development. They reported that students developed very good comprehension skills in French, but that there were gaps and inaccuracies in their spoken and written French that would not be expected in the French of native speakers their own age.

Other researchers also reported on the ways in which students' use of French was different from the target. For example, Harley & Swain (1984) found that after several years in CBLT, immersion students made systematic errors, including errors in the use of common verbs, grammatical gender marking, and word order in sentences and prepositional phrases. Furthermore, researchers observed that students seemed to reach a plateau in their acquisition of French and that once that plateau was reached, there were few significant changes in the accuracy of their language use (Genesee, 1987; Lyster, 1987). Nor did immersion students acquire the ability to use language easily and appropriately in informal settings (Mougeon, Nadasdi, & Rehner, 2010). In contrast to the observation that minority-language students had usually acquired BICS skills after a couple of years, immersion students were more likely to acquire a sort of classroom variety of French that was neither like the informal language of French L1 children nor the more formal academic language of their teachers and textbooks (Calvé, 1986).

Comprehensible input is a starting point for language learning, but it is clear from research in a variety of CBLT contexts that learning the language requires a focus and an effort that is specific. That is, even if students understand their teachers and their textbook material well enough to succeed on measures of academic content knowledge, it cannot be assumed that the language will 'take care of itself.'

Spotlight Study 3.3

In a study of lessons in two school districts in the USA, Short (2002) observed the extent to which teachers' discourse focused on content, language, or task management. She looked at four teachers teaching sheltered social studies classes at the middle school level. Two had been trained as ESL teachers and two as social studies teachers. In transcripts containing over 3,000 teacher utterances, she found an average of 20 percent focused on language, 35 percent on the content, and 44 percent on task procedures. A similar pattern was observed in the teachers' lesson plans. Both the ESL-trained teachers and those without that training tended to give very little attention to language itself. When they did pay attention to language, 95 percent of that focus was on vocabulary rather than on any other aspect of language use. Short concludes that teachers need better preparation for teaching language itself and that they need to be persuaded of the importance of including explicit focus on language as part of every sheltered content lesson.

The research reported in this article formed an important background to the development of an approach to professional development for sheltered instruction that is designed to help teachers integrate language and content (Echevarria, Vogt, & Short, 2012). Some of the main ideas of that approach are introduced in this article. One of the central principles is the importance of including explicit language-focused objectives in each lesson. That is, in every lesson plan, both the teacher and the students should have a clear idea of what language they need to learn as well as what the content objectives are. ■

There are still differences of opinion about how to provide for both content and language instruction in CBLT contexts. In nearly all program types—for both minority- and majority-language children—the emphasis tends to be on the necessity of mastering the content, and the range of expectations for language achievement is quite varied, as are students' proficiency outcomes. Focusing on foreign language immersion research, Lyster (2007) is among those who argue that the goals of CBLT must include language proficiency, not just for understanding the content, but for its own sake, in light of the amount of effort that goes into learning academic content in L2.

> If second language learning were not a primary goal of immersion and content-based instruction, then it would be much easier for children to engage with the school curriculum entirely through their first language. To justify the extra effort required of all stakeholders associated with programs promoting curricular instruction in more than one language, including teachers and students alike, learning the additional language needs to be a primary objective.
>
> (Lyster, 2007, p. 6)

Expectations for the language development of minority-language students tend to be very high. Indeed, in many situations, the goal for them is the achievement of native-like proficiency that allows them to use language in ways that make them seem indistinguishable from their peers who have never spoken another language. Reaching that kind of proficiency is very demanding, and it is important for teachers, students, parents, and policy-makers to understand that it takes time, effort, and instruction that includes focus on language itself. We have seen that minority-language students in mainstream settings may develop the kind of socially fluent and appropriate use of language that is difficult for majority-language students in foreign language settings—including immersion. However, they may lag in their development of the vocabulary and style they need for more advanced academic work. How can CBLT be implemented in ways that increase students' skills in the language itself?

Access to comprehensible input in content-based instruction can get things started. However, educators who have worked to understand and implement CBLT have concluded that there are considerable risks in assuming that students will learn the language as long as they are able to understand the content. Many studies show that students can spend years in CBLT classrooms where they perform well on assessments of content knowledge but where their use of the second language shows gaps in accuracy and appropriateness. Such gaps may be attributable to the absence of certain features in the language used in the classroom. In one of the earliest publications drawing attention to this, Swain (1988) observed that in history lessons in French immersion programs, where one might expect to find many uses of past tense verbs, teachers often adopted the historical present, describing events in a style that is perfectly appropriate and correct, but which does not provide students with opportunities to hear and learn a major verb form. This led her to conclude that content teaching is not necessarily good language teaching.

Lyster (2007) reviews several studies that reveal the relative rarity of particular language features during CBLT lessons in French immersion, including the basic verb tenses. Without the evidence from transcripts of classroom recordings, we would probably just assume that students would have plenty of chances to learn, for example, the past tense. However, researchers found that only about 15 percent of the verbs students heard were in the past tense.

Other studies have also identified gaps in the language students acquire in CBLT classrooms without some systematic attention to making language itself a focus of students' learning. Lyster (1994) found that students who had spent years in CBLT instruction in French immersion had not internalized the rules for using *tu* and *vous*, the informal and formal second person pronouns. From the evidence, the classroom context simply provided too few examples of this contrast to allow students to 'pick it up' during their content-based instruction. It was only when the feature was explicitly taught and practiced in contextualized activities that they made substantial progress on using it correctly.

Such findings suggest that without intentional and systematic focus on language features, learners in CBLT classes may simply not have enough exposure to certain forms that are infrequent in classroom discourse. In addition, as we saw in Chapter 2, they may have difficulty with some language features such as markers of grammatical gender which, although present in substantial numbers, are difficult to notice because they are not salient in oral language and are redundant—providing little or no meaning that cannot be gleaned from the main words in the sentence. Good examples of this for English are the simple present and simple past verb endings (My friend want*s* to go to the store. Last year, my mom cook*ed* a big turkey for Thanksgiving.) Even when these forms are present in sentences that students hear or read, they are hard to notice without some explicit attention to them.

Classroom Snapshot 3.3

My son learned French in a variety of CBLT programs at school (including some time in a French school and in partial immersion). In Grade 6, he asked me to help him proofread a book report on a novel he had read in French. The report referred to a story about two boys who worked together with their karate master to solve a mystery. In going to the book to check something, I discovered that the book was actually about a boy and a girl who were friends, but my son had never noticed the numerous feminine pronouns and adjective agreements related to the girl in the story.

(Lightbown, 1990, p. 89)

In experimental studies several researchers have explored the effectiveness of language-focused instruction and feedback in classrooms where young children are engaged in CBLT. Having identified language features that students have difficulty with or that do not appear to develop fully in meaning-focused content-based lessons, the researchers, often working collaboratively with teachers, have introduced language-focused instruction on some particular language feature and then assessed the impact of this intervention in students' developing knowledge and use of the language features in focus.

It has been widely documented that English-speaking learners of French, including those in immersion, make frequent errors in marking the gender of nouns (Lyster, 2007). In her research with Grade 2 immersion students, Harley (1998) sought to deal with the fact that gender marking lacks salience and can appear to be arbitrary. She designed instructional materials that were meant to make the grammatical gender of nouns more salient and to lead learners to an awareness that the way a noun is spelled or the way it sounds is a hint as to its gender. Using variations on familiar games, songs, and rhymes, students were led to pay attention to gender. For example, in 'Simon says', performing the required gesture depended on noticing whether the noun was masculine or feminine.

The students in the experimental group improved in their ability to hear and produce the markers of grammatical gender on nouns. However, while they were fairly accurate in marking familiar nouns, they had not improved in their ability to generalize the pattern of spelling as a clue to gender. Nevertheless, in interviews, some of the students could actually describe the pattern, even though they did not always apply this knowledge in their own language production. As we saw in Chapter 2, to go from a stage where they know what the pattern is to a stage at which they use it consistently and automatically, students need both practice and consistent feedback, especially feedback that calls on them to retrieve the correct form in the context of meaning-focused use.

Harley's research shows that even very young students can benefit from language-focused learning. Other researchers have also found that primary school learners are able to make progress in interlanguage development when they receive such focused instruction within the overall context of CBLT instruction (Lyster, 2004; Serrano, 2011).

Activity 3.2

Imagine that one of your students is Luz, a 10-year-old girl who has just moved to the US from Mexico. Before moving, her family had some problems that made it difficult for her to attend school as regularly as they would have liked. Thus, she can read a little bit in Spanish, but her academic subject matter knowledge is not at the level it would be if she had attended school regularly. Look at the excerpt on p.92 from a Grade 3 textbook designed for teaching ELL students about science.

What language features do you think Luz will need help with? What features do you think will be easy for her? Do you think it helps you help her if you know some Spanish? How would you help her get the most from this text? Think of both what you might do and how Luz could get help from other students, as well as things that she could do on her own.

How People Affect the Environment

An environment is all the things that surround a living thing. Trees, water, and land are part of the environment.

When people change the environment, they usually change the homes of plants and animals. If they cut down a tree, the squirrels and birds who lived in that tree lose their homes.

Even though an animal's home may change, it can still survive. An animal needs food, water, and shelter. It also needs air and space. An animal can move to a new environment and get what it needs.

(Chamot et al., 1997)

Now imagine that another student in your class is Nguyen, whose school history is similar to the one described for Luz (limited schooling up to age 10, basic literacy in his home language). His home language is Vietnamese, a language you are not familiar with and one that is not related to English. How would your approach to helping him with this text be different from your approach with Luz? What would be similar in your approach?

Group-Work in Language Learning

We have seen that cooperative learning can be effective for content learning. However, it is sometimes suggested that having students work in groups or pairs will not be an effective practice with regard to furthering language development. Some teachers fear that students will provide each other with poor language models and be unable to correct each other's errors. Teachers worry that students may not find the language resources needed to complete tasks and that they will become discouraged or frustrated. Another concern is that if students share the same L1, they will revert to using that language rather than sustaining the effort required to use the second/foreign language. These are legitimate concerns, but the potential advantages of group-work greatly outweigh the disadvantages if tasks are well planned, students are well prepared, and the language requirements are within their proficiency range.

Classroom Snapshot 3.4 comes from the same Grade 5 classroom in the USA that we saw in Spotlight Study 3.1. It provides some examples of how ELLs with different proficiency levels can work together in ways that promote learning for all of them. The students are working in groups to understand a reading passage on human anatomy and to complete a task related to the passage. They are using the approach called Collaborative Strategic Reading that was introduced in Spotlight Study 3.1. As we saw in that study, each student has a particular role to play in completing the task. One aspect of this reading approach is to identify each 'click and clunk', that is, language or concepts that they do not understand. As you read Classroom Snapshot 3.4, keep the following questions in mind:

- Do the students seem to be focused on the content of the reading passage?
- Do you think they have understood what they read?
- Are they able to help each other?
- How do the students make use of their Spanish?
- What do you think about the fact that they pause to talk about a cognate word that looks almost identical in English and Spanish?

Classroom Snapshot 3.4

Note: When students speak Spanish, a translation of what they say is shown in square brackets.

Mario: Does anybody have any click and clunks? *¿Alguien tiene alguna palabra que no entiende?* [Does anyone have a word they don't understand?] OK, do you know what voluntary is?

Frank: *Voluntario?*

Mario: *¿Sí, que quiere decir?* [Yes, what does it mean?]

Frank: *Como ellos se mueven cuando ellos quieren.* [That they move when they want.]

Gloria: What Frank is trying to say is that voluntary means when all your fingers move by themselves, that is because of the muscle cells. When a part of your body moves when you want it to and it stops when you want it to.

(From Klingner & Vaughn, 2000, pp. 83–4)

In Classroom Snapshot 3.4, the students do seem to be focused on the content of the reading passage, and they seem quite clear about using the group discussion to ensure that every member of the group has an opportunity to understand the text. One has the impression that the students have been well prepared for their group activity and that they have a clear understanding of their task. Klingner and Vaughn's discussion in the journal article from which this example is taken provides confirmation of this impression.

Students' use of Spanish is quite interesting. This brief conversation suggests that Frank's English skills are less advanced than those of Mario and Gloria. Frank uses Spanish to suggest the meaning of a word. Mario seems to use it to make sure that Frank understands and that he is included in the conversation. Gloria, in this excerpt, does not actually speak Spanish, but her understanding of it gives Frank a great learning opportunity by confirming that what he said was correct and providing the English words to say what he meant. Of course, she goes beyond translating what he said and extends his idea, using both academic language and informal language to confirm what they know about what allows fingers to move voluntarily.

It is striking that, even though no one cited 'voluntary' as a problematic word, Mario felt it was important to make sure it was understood. On the one hand, that may seem odd since it is a word that is nearly identical in English and Spanish, but there are two reasons why the time spent on this may be worthwhile. First, research has shown that second language learners do not always recognize cognates as words that they know. This is particularly true when they hear rather than read them, but it can also be true when the spelling of the two words is not identical. Second, the fact that Frank offered *voluntario* does not mean that he knew its meaning or understood what it meant in the context of this anatomy lesson. Thus, the discussion of this word may have the double benefit of helping Frank learn the meaning of the word in Spanish as well as in English.

In dual immersion classrooms, students from both majority and minority groups are learning a second language. In principle, these classes have the unique benefit of placing students together with peers who are native speakers of the language they are learning, providing them with natural native speaker input to their language development. In practice, it cannot be assumed that this benefit will be equally available to the minority- and majority-group students. Several studies have confirmed that the majority language tends to predominate in interactions among students themselves, whether in the academic activities of the classroom or in the social interactions in other settings (for example, Christian et al., 1997).

Ballinger & Lyster (2011) found that students in an English/Spanish dual immersion program in the US used far more English than Spanish in all activities other than those that were directed by the teacher in the Spanish classroom. They also found, however, that a number of factors influenced the likelihood that students would speak Spanish, for example, when students accommodated to the needs of Spanish-speaking newcomers. Perhaps most important, the students' behaviors and their attitudes toward the importance of speaking Spanish were influenced by the extent to which their teachers were consistent in their own use of Spanish and how much they encouraged both Spanish L1 and Spanish L2 students to use that language during classroom activities.

Hickey (2001) observed the choice of language by preschool children attending Irish medium schools in the Republic of Ireland. In this context, the goal of the educational program is to increase the number of Irish speakers in an environment where English is often dominant. She found that students tended to speak English more than Irish to each other, even though the classes included students who spoke Irish or both Irish and English, as well as some who spoke only English at home. In classroom activities, children from Irish-speaking homes spoke Irish just over half the time. Fewer than a third of the utterances produced by students from bilingual or English-only homes were in Irish. In light of the fact that the aim of the Irish-medium schools is to develop students' proficiency in Irish, Hickey asks, understandably, 'Who is immersing whom?' She points out that the desire to increase the number of Irish L2 speakers should 'not short-change the [Irish] L1 speakers, who need language maintenance' (p. 470).

The presence of peers who speak each language can be somewhat complicated in other ways as well. Lightbown (2007) observed classes in a Spanish–English dual immersion program in a school in a low-income neighborhood in a US city. The English-dominant students in this school were almost all African American and speakers of a variety of English that is characteristic of their community. They were faced with the challenge of learning both Spanish and the variety of English that is considered appropriate in academic settings. The Spanish speakers also faced an interesting challenge. Clearly, they were expected to learn the English spoken by their teachers, but it was also in their interest to learn the variety of English spoken by their classmates.

The European Schools also offer an opportunity to look at the influence of the wider social context. Housen (2002a,b) reports on studies of the L2 English language skill of students in European Schools where English was the language of the wider environment (that is, the school was located in England) and in schools where the language was not spoken in the community (that is, schools in other European countries). The study compared the English lexical and grammatical knowledge of elementary school students who had experienced English language learning in three types of settings: typical foreign language instruction in Italy, European School education in Italy or Belgium, and European School education in England.

After students had been in these programs for a total of 250 hours, the researchers found a very large effect on all measures for the location of the school. Overall, the researchers found more advanced grammatical knowledge (though not more advanced vocabulary) for students in the European Schools than for those in the more typical foreign language instruction, but it was the status of English outside the school that had the greatest effect on students' performance after 250 hours of school-based learning. That is, students whose school was in England were more advanced than those whose school was in a country where English was a foreign language. Housen and his colleagues continued this line of research with older students and we will return to their studies when we look at secondary school students in Chapter 4.

Vocabulary Learning

As we saw in Chapter 2, vocabulary is a key element of successful reading and academic learning. New vocabulary is learned gradually, and learners usually need many encounters with a word before they learn it. Reading has been cited as the primary source of new vocabulary knowledge. This is partly because, even in classroom interaction, oral language tends to use a very high proportion of the most frequent words in the language, with relatively few occurrences of words drawn from low-frequency words. Thus, it is possible to hear a great deal of language without having access to the range of words needed in academic work. Indeed, as we shall see in looking at Spotlight Study 3.4, reading may not always provide exposure to this language either.

Spotlight Study 3.4

Gardner (2004, 2008) has emphasized the importance of reading different text types in order to encounter low-frequency academic words often enough to learn them. In analyzing authentic texts written for school-aged students, he looked at how often readers might encounter new words and at whether these words occur often enough that readers might be able to learn them from their reading. That is, leaving aside high-frequency words that the reader would most likely know already, he analyzed the occurrence and the frequency of possible learning targets in narrative (fiction) and expository (non-fiction informational) texts.

Gardner found that three quarters of the target words occurred either in narrative text only or in expository texts only. This was true, even when Gardner intentionally chose books that touched on the same theme. Thus, for example, readers of an expository text about mummies might encounter words such as *embalmed*, *bacteria*, and *quarry*, but even when mummies figured in the plot of the narrative texts, readers might not encounter these words. Indeed a surprisingly small number of words in the narrative texts were related to the theme. Instead, there were more words such as *suddenly*, *finally*, or *interrupted* that moved the narrative along. In addition, in analyzing texts of the same length from narrative and expository writing aimed at students at Grades 5–6, he found fewer low-frequency words overall in the narrative texts.

Second language learners need to learn both low-frequency and high-frequency words, and Gardner suggests that the latter are the types of words students will encounter in a variety of texts, with a fair possibility of learning them. However, he cautions that students will be more likely to encounter multiple repetitions of words drawn from 'the vocabulary of school' if they are exposed to 'narrow reading of theme-related expository materials' (2008, p. 111). He concludes that 'more attention should be paid to the *what* of reading and vocabulary exposure, not merely to the *how much*' (2008, p. 112).

Lest it seem that there is no role for more extensive, less focused reading, including narrative fiction, Gardner suggests that such reading can contribute to the development of fluency and automaticity because of the recurrence of so many high-frequency words that appear in a variety of texts. ■

We have seen that the challenge of learning vocabulary is a major key to success in reading comprehension. It is another example of the need to provide students with some direct language-focused teaching rather than waiting for them to catch up with the moving target through meaning-focused activities alone. As Beck et al. (2002) suggest, students will benefit from 'robust vocabulary instruction' that can speed their acquisition of some of the hundreds of words they need to learn each year.

Corrective Feedback and Language-Focused Learning

As we saw in Chapter 2, the role of feedback on error has been seen as an essential part of language-focused learning. In a study that has inspired much discussion and follow up research, Lyster & Ranta (1997) analyzed the feedback patterns of teachers during content-based lessons in French immersion classes. In transcripts from over 18 hours of regular classroom interaction involving four different teachers, they identified opportunities for teachers to respond to errors in students' oral production and analyzed both the teachers' feedback on these errors and students' responses to the feedback.

Of more than 3200 multi-word student utterances in the classroom transcripts, approximately one-third contained some error—a problem with vocabulary, grammar, pronunciation, or some other aspect of language use. Lyster & Ranta found that teachers responded to about 60 percent of these by providing some kind of feedback that an observer would recognize as corrective. More than half of these feedback responses were in the form of recasts, that is, a repetition of what the student had said, but with the error corrected. For three of the four teachers, the recasts made up 60 percent or more of the feedback responses. None of the five other feedback types came close. For example, only 8 percent of the feedback responses included metalinguistic information such as, 'Is that how we say it in French?' and 7 percent explicitly told the student that an error had occurred before providing the correct form, 'You should say …'.

The finding that has generated the most interest is the frequency with which students responded to the teachers' corrective feedback. Overall students showed some sign of recognizing that the teacher had offered corrective feedback just over half the time. The feedback that was least likely to lead to a student trying again and getting it right was the recast. More than two thirds of the time, students did not indicate that they had noticed the teacher's feedback that was offered in the form of a recast.

In a follow-up study, Lyster (1998) observed another interesting phenomenon. In content-based French immersion lessons, teachers appeared to use repetition of a student's correct speech and a recast of a student's error in almost exactly the same way. Furthermore, comments such as, 'Right' or 'Good' that appear to evaluate the student's utterance were equally likely to accompany recasts of incorrect utterances and repetitions of correct ones. Such similarity would appear to make it difficult for students to recognize a recast as corrective. They might hear it as a confirmation of what they have said rather than as a reaction to how they said it. Lyster & Ranta did not conclude that recasts should not be used. Rather, they suggested that teachers use a greater variety of feedback types—increasing the frequency of those that are likely to be noticed more often by learners.

Oliver & Mackey (2003) found that teachers in Australian primary school classes with ELL students offered feedback on language use in different ways according to the type of classroom activity. They found that teachers offered the least feedback on language errors during meaning-focused activities, including content lessons, classroom management, and communicative interaction. They were most likely to offer feedback when the lesson was on language itself, providing another example of the tendency in CBLT for teachers to see language and content as separate instructional goals (Fazio & Lyster, 1998; Short, 2002).

Lyster & Mori (2006) have suggested that in classes where teachers and students focus primarily on meaning (the case in French immersion classes), feedback in the form of prompts is more likely to be noticed by students. In contrast, for students who are accustomed to instruction in which there is greater focus on language itself (the case in some Japanese immersion classes), students are more likely to recognize recasts as feedback on a language error. They propose the counterbalance hypothesis: in classrooms where students are accustomed to instruction that focuses on language form, recasts are noticed more readily; in contexts where teachers tend to focus primarily on meaning, recasts are often interpreted as the teacher's confirmation of a student's meaning rather than as a suggested correction of language form.

Perhaps the most significant inference we can draw from these studies and from the counterbalance hypothesis is that students may benefit from a variety of feedback types according to the overall classroom environment. We have seen that language errors in CBLT do not typically get consistent feedback from teachers. Placing this in the framework of Nation's Four Strands, we can understand that in meaning-focused activities, teachers and students seem to pay little explicit attention to language. To a certain extent, this is a positive finding. In order to develop confidence and positive motivation, students need to feel that what is most important is what they are saying rather than whether they are saying it in error-free sentences. However, this does not mean that feedback cannot be integrated into meaning-focused activities.

Language-focused activities that introduce some new language feature or which require some extended explanation to help students see why they are making a certain error may work best when they are offered separately from content-based instruction, allowing students to give their full attention to the way the language works. However, corrective feedback and other kinds of language-focused input can also work well during meaning-focused activities, if they:

1 focus on only a small number of language features in a given lesson or task
2 focus on something students already know but don't always do
3 are explicit enough to ensure that students recognize what the teacher is reacting to
4 do not interrupt the overall flow of meaning-focused interaction.

(Lightbown, 1998)

Activity 3.3

Look at the notes you took in response to the questions in Activity 3.1. Now that you have read about research with young learners, can you answer those questions more fully? Can you support your answers by drawing on the research? Have any of your answers changed? Do you feel that some of the questions cannot be answered on the basis of what you have read? Can you suggest how answers to those questions might be found through research?

Summary

Both content learning and language learning in the early school years start when students have access to comprehensible input from their peers, their teachers, and instructional materials. In addition, opportunities to observe and interact with the teacher and with other students can push their learning forward. With the development of oral language ability, students prepare for the challenge of acquiring literacy skills. These skills are crucial in preparing children to continue learning through reading as they progress in school. Both majority- and minority-language students face considerable challenges in these first years of L2 learning, but in a supportive environment, they can learn the skills they need for the greater challenges that lie ahead. In secondary school, they will need to continue developing their academic language abilities as well as content knowledge in a greater range of subjects.

4 Classroom-Based Research on CBLT with Adolescent Learners

Preview

In this chapter, we will explore the CBLT experiences of students aged 12–18 years. We will see how the learning opportunities and the academic demands for secondary school students are different from those of the younger learners we read about in Chapter 3. We will link the classroom research to the research covered in Chapter 2, including the question of how students' age is related to long-term success in L2 learning.

What Do Students Need to Learn in Secondary School?

For adolescents who are working in a second language, the demands and expectations for both language proficiency and academic learning in the secondary school are substantial. Their success in school depends on being able to read for information, understand teachers' instructional language, and demonstrate their knowledge and understanding of subject matter—both orally and in writing.

For students in the secondary school years, academic material can be complex and unrelated to experiences in their daily lives. They must be able to recognize and remember what they have learned previously, but they must also make connections to information that may not have been explicitly taught. If students' language proficiency is not yet at an age-appropriate level, the linguistic register and vocabulary density of textbooks and primary source materials will make them difficult to read. Teachers' classroom presentations may be hard to follow. And producing history papers or science reports can seem overwhelming.

A student who is doing academic work at the secondary school level needs to know thousands of words. As we saw in Chapter 2, this includes not only the 2000 or so most frequent words that make up 80 percent of most texts. They must also learn academic words—both those that are common to a wide range of disciplines and those that are particular to specific disciplines.

We also saw in Chapter 2 and Chapter 3 that there are important reasons to be cautious about relying too much on incidental vocabulary learning, especially for second language learners.

While vocabulary is a crucial part of learning academic language, there are many other features of language that must also be learned (Scarcella, 2011). Shin (2009) describes a series of activities she carried out with ELL high school students from a variety of different L1 backgrounds. She worked with them on understanding and constructing the kinds of complex sentences that occurred in the news magazines that they read together, making the case that grammar was an important part of both comprehension and production and that language form and language meaning are inextricable.

> By raising specific questions about the students' own grammatical and rhetorical choices, I tried to help them see that grammar is not simply a set of rules to be memorized, but a result of deliberate attempts to convey the intended meanings of the writers.
>
> (Shin, 2009, p. 398)

Learning academic language at the secondary school level also involves learning new ways of thinking, ways that students may have little experience with outside the classroom. Zwiers (2006) describes the challenges faced by ELL students in learning academic language and ways of thinking as they move from primary school to the higher grades:

> Much more complex than a list of words and phrases to memorize, academic language embodies the cognitive, linguistic, cultural, and discipline-specific features of discourse found in school and beyond—in scientific, business, and other technical arenas. This is a double challenge for many students who are learning not only another language but also an academic dialect of that language. Closely related to issues of language are the dimensions of academic thinking: the ways in which experts from various disciplines approach their research and argumentation.
>
> (Zwiers, 2006, pp. 317–18)

Look at the interaction in Classroom Snapshot 4.1. Do you see opportunities for students to acquire academic language and ways of thinking?

Classroom Snapshot 4.1

This science lesson is being taught in an English immersion program in a middle school in China.

T: First of all, er, I have a riddle for you, and let's see who can guess what it is. Er, it's a kind of liquid, but it has no smell, color or taste. What's that?

Ss: [Many students call out] Water!

T: So you all agree that it is water, right?
Ss: Yeah.
T: That is what we are going to learn in this period. OK, so we are going to learn something about water.
[later in the lesson]
T: What is water used for? What do you use water? XXX [naming a student] please.
S: We can use water for drink.
T: For drinking. You use water for drinking only? And you use water for washing your face. Thank you.
S: We use water to make electricity.
T: What can we use? For making electricity. OK good.
S: Taking shower.
T: Complete sentence. We can use water for taking shower. Or to take shower. XXX [naming another student] please. [...]
S: The water can use for eat, clean.
T: So water is used for cleaning the places. Yes.

(Hoare, 2010, pp. 79, 82)

From this brief excerpt, there seems little evidence that the teacher is focusing on the development of academic English or scientific thinking about the topic. Rather, the emphasis seems to be on more conversational interaction. Is this just the teacher's way of getting students to start thinking about the topic? Or is this an example of CBLT where, instead of finding ways to help students engage with academic content, the teacher does not get beyond simplified language *and* content? We will return to a discussion of Classroom Snapshot 4.1 later in this chapter.

Learning the Content in CBLT

There is ample evidence that minority-language students often experience difficulty in meeting the academic demands of secondary schools. For recently arrived minority-language students, especially those who have limited education and literacy in their L1 as well as limited proficiency in L2, the educational challenges at the secondary level can prove so difficult that they drop out of school or fail to pass required tests. Even for ELL students who have had most of their education in US schools, performance on academic achievement measures is sometimes disappointing and dropout rates are high.

Majority-language students who have spent years in immersion classes may feel pressure to return to a focus on studies in the L1, in anticipation of examinations and out of concern about being ready for university studies in their L1. Internationally, students who have received some of their academic instruction in a foreign language have sometimes performed less well on their subject matter examinations than those who have studied those subjects in their L1, leading to questions about the efficacy of CBLT for content learning.

In their review of research on academic achievement in different types of educational programs for ELL students in the US, Lindholm-Leary & Borsato (2006) comment about the lack of 'empirical research on instructional strategies or approaches to teaching content' (p. 190). Their review of the studies that did look at relationships between teaching and learning outcomes led them to observe several things about effective teaching for ELLs. What the effective approaches had in common included the use of specialized materials that were accessible to the learners, an interactive–dialogic style of teaching (rather than teacher-centered transmission style), a greater number of cognitively challenging questions, and well-structured cooperative group-work.

In the following section, we will look at some of the studies that have been done with learners in various CBLT contexts, finding approaches that have led students to successful learning of academic content and others that have been less effective.

Classroom Snapshot 4.2

Students in this class in a middle school in China are learning to classify animals in a CBLT science class. The conversation below is one of several that the teacher has with individual students as they work on their own classifications.

T: OK, so XXX [student's name], would you please repeat your classification?
S1: Living, er, things with wings can be classified into two groups. One is, the first group is can't fly.
T: Oh, the first group is the things that can't fly. OK?
S1: The second group is the things, er,
T: That ...
S1: That can fly.
T: Can fly. OK?
S1: The, the penguin is, the penguin can't fly.
T: The penguin can't fly, so it belongs to this group. And?
S1: Er, the thing that can fly can be classified into two groups. One is living things and another group is non-living things.
[...]

T: Non-living things. OK. So what is the non-living thing?
S1: A plane.
T: A plane, yes. A plane is the non-living thing. And for living things?
S1: Er, living things can be classified into two groups. One is, the first group is invertebrates and the second group is vertebrates. Er, in, invertebrates can be classified … er, the butterfly is invertebrates.
T: Butterfly belongs to this group. OK?
S1: Vertebrate, er, vertebrates, birds is the vertebrates. The birds can, and penguin.
T: Penguin …
S1: Birds and mammals are vertebrates. Penguin is birds.
T: Penguin?
Ss: Pigeon.
S1: Pigeon is birds.
T: A pigeon belongs to this group and?
S1: Bat is mammals.

(Kong & Hoare, 2011, p. 320)

There are many things to notice about Classroom Snapshot 4.2. For example, the teacher accepts the student's responses and then invites further elaboration, which the student is able to provide. Rather than provide answers by using recasts (that is, by providing the correct form), the teacher tends to draw the answer from the student by using prompts, trying to get the learner to self-correct. The student, whose English is not very advanced, is able to succeed because the task is well defined and the student has been prepared for it. There are some errors in the student's grammar, but the teacher remains focused on the use of the scientific language of classification, both the vocabulary and the phrases that are appropriate for this context, for example, '… can be classified into two groups.'

Classroom Snapshots 4.1 and 4.2 come from research by Kong and Hoare (2011), who studied how 'cognitive content engagement' creates opportunities for students to learn language and content in CBLT classes in several middle schools in China. They found a considerable range of language and content teaching in different classes. They observed the teacher in Classroom Snapshot 4.1, who focused on getting students engaged in conversation that mostly used everyday language that they were already familiar with rather than fully exploiting the scientific content of the lesson or pushing students to acquire new academic language or content. Hoare (2010) comments on what else they saw in the lesson taught by the teacher in Classroom Snapshot 4.1:

> Throughout the lesson, there is no focus on specific language forms. The new English which the class acquires appears to be incidental, unplanned and unexploited rather than drawn purposely from the content. ... It is clear that this lesson has no language learning objectives derived from content learning objectives, which Kong (2008) and Snow, Met and Genesee (1989) have proposed as necessary for successful CBLT lessons. This lesson cannot be said to be a successful CBLT lesson.
>
> (Hoare, 2010, p. 82)

In contrast, the teacher in Classroom Snapshot 4.2 came to the lesson with clear objectives for expanding students' knowledge of both academic content and academic language. She used language that was 'content obligatory' and 'content compatible' (Met, 1994; Snow, Met, & Genesee, 1989), and she focused on expanding students' knowledge of the scientific content, in this case, the classification of vertebrates. The following summary of an interview makes it clear that this teacher knew what she wanted students to accomplish.

> ... the teacher said that she wanted the students to 'learn how to classify things by their physical features. That is the content objective: to use their brain to think. I want them to learn more about science.' There is a corresponding focus on the academic 'language of' and 'language for' classification. She said, 'for English objective, they have to learn "can be classified", "breathe with lung or gills", lay eggs to reproduce" or "give birth to babies to reproduce".'
>
> (Kong & Hoare, 2011, p. 318)

The longer transcript from which the lesson in Classroom Snapshot 4.2 is taken shows that the planning and specifying of objectives for content and language inform her teaching and the students' learning. The lesson is cyclical, in the sense that there is a series of activities that includes a range of opportunities to work on the new language and content—classroom oral interaction to a final written text—allowing students multiple encounters with the new material, thus increasing the chances that they will remember it later (see also Kong, 2009).

Hoare (2010) has observed that in some of the schools where CBLT is being implemented in China, teachers' expertise and academic resources are quite limited. One result of this, for example, is the recruitment of English teachers to teach academic content in subjects for which they do not have expertise or of teachers with adequate academic knowledge who are not prepared to teach in English. Nevertheless, Hoare points out how even less than ideal CBLT lessons can enrich the English learning experience of students in China, where instruction is typically 'teacher-centered and dominated by grammar teaching towards grammar-based assessments' (p. 82). Hoare sees the experiments in CBLT as a step in the right direction toward expanding learning opportunities to the majority of students in China who attend regular public schools.

Activity 4.1

Based on the information you have from Classroom Snapshot 4.2 and the teacher's interview, do you think this teacher's instructional practices are providing students with contexts for learning through all of Nation's four strands described in Chapter 2? Give examples of how you think the teacher is providing opportunities for different strands.

The students in Classroom Snapshots 4.1 and 4.2 are speakers of Chinese, learning English, a language that is quite distant from their L1. This means that they cannot rely on cognates or similarities in language patterns such as word order or types of grammatical markers to help them with the new language. They have acquired literacy skills and academic content in their L1, and they have learned how to learn in a school setting. Even though English represents a substantial learning challenge, they seem well prepared to use their prior academic skills in meeting it.

Classroom Snapshot 4.3 also comes from a classroom where students' L1 is not at all related to their L2. It is a Grade 10 classroom in an Inuit community in northern Quebec, Canada—the same community where we met the Grade 3 teacher in Classroom Snapshot 3.2. The students are about 15 years old. Their first language is Inuktitut, which is the language spoken among most adult Inuit in the community.

Although they had some initial literacy training in their L1, most of the students' education has been provided through their second language. Beyond Grade 3, students have all academic courses in either French or English, according to their parents' choice. The parents of the students in this classroom have chosen French. Other students in the same school are being educated through English, which is spoken a little more widely than French in their community. Some of the students have learned some English informally, but they have not experienced CBLT in that language. The challenges for them in learning to read French and learning subject matter through that language are especially great, both because of the great linguistic distance between Inuktitut and French and because the students do not have advanced oral proficiency in French. As you read the transcript in Classroom Snapshot 4.3, keep following questions in mind:

- What is the teacher doing to help the students understand the subject matter?
- What else do you think he could do?
- Do you think the teacher could take advantage of the fact that most students also know some English? Do you think he should?
- How could students get more from this text after the teacher has read it with them?
- What do you think students will remember from this part of the lesson?

Classroom Snapshot 4.3

The lesson is about beluga whales. The teacher reads the italicized sentence from the students' textbook; the remaining material comes from the teacher himself.

> OK page 56 ... *In the estuaries, fresh water from the rivers mixes with salt water from the ocean and the warmth of the water in the estuaries enhances the lactation of the mother beluga.* What is warmth? [no answer] We have cold water, we have cold water ... we have hot water, we have warm water [showing the relationship with his hands]. Warm is between cold and hot. So, warm water in the estuaries allows the mother beluga, the mama, to have, how shall I say this, lactation, which has to do with milk. OK. Like mothers, like us here, have milk in their breasts for babies, so, mother belugas have the same system. OK. So, that enables them to have more milk, more easily, since the water is warm. Are you with me? OK. Page 54.

(Translated from French transcripts based on recorded classroom observations. Spada & Lightbown, 2002, p. 235)

The teacher in Classroom Snapshot 4.3 seems to be aware of a number of places where students might not know the meaning of important words in the text. For example, since no one offers an answer to his question 'What is warmth?' he uses words the students do know (cold and hot) and gestures to show where 'warm' fits on the temperature continuum. To help explain the meaning of the term *lactation* he again uses words he expects the students to know and makes the comparison with human mothers and their babies. Aware that some of the students also have some knowledge of English, he sometimes draws on that knowledge to help them understand a text, but he does not do so in this example. It should be noted that, in this educational context, teachers make a great effort to promote students' use of French, and this is likely to limit their use of English in classroom language.

If students are to remember the new vocabulary and the concepts from this lesson, they will need opportunities to encounter them many more times. Ideally, students will have opportunities not only to understand the words when the teacher uses them but also to say or write something that includes these ideas and connects them with other things that they have already learned—whether in school or elsewhere. For example, with regard to this lesson on beluga whales, the teacher might make connections to the students' personal knowledge and cultural heritage. The lesson comes from a textbook that has been developed for this population and thus includes topics that have some importance in the local community.

As he proceeds in this lesson, the teacher might get students engaged in a group task, for example, creating a chart that compares the information about beluga whales to information they can find about other arctic animals. He might have students write new words in vocabulary notebooks, or prepare an oral report on the belugas' migration patterns and their feeding habits. Students might write a report on what they can learn about the status of belugas as an endangered species, bringing local cultural knowledge into the discussion by interviewing family members or hunters. Fluency development might be encouraged by having students prepare a story, poem, or 'news minute' about the beluga whales for presentation to younger students in the school.

The kind of learning that stays with us requires that we encounter something numerous times, in different contexts, using different kinds of processing—reading a text, interviewing elders in the community, writing a story, or making a poster—and that we have experience in retrieving it from our memory when it is no longer present in the environment—for example, answering questions in a game or on a test. The fragment of a lesson in Classroom Snapshot 4.3 is just the beginning of an experience that will add to students' knowledge of beluga whales and the French language vocabulary and language patterns to express that knowledge and relate it to other knowledge.

One approach that has been found effective for teaching content subjects in ways that also further language development is based on *systemic functional linguistics*. This approach to language study is based on the work of Halliday (2004), whose linguistic theory emphasizes how language makes meaning. Schleppegrell & de Oliveira describe a project in which the goal was 'to help history teachers understand the challenges of their discipline in linguistic terms through a functional approach to grammar that foregrounds meaning' (2006, p. 255). In that project, the researchers worked with teachers in high school history classes, with the goal of helping them help students understand the content by better understanding how the language conveys that content.

Schleppegrell & de Oliveira emphasize that the history teachers did not have a great deal of experience or preparation for working with the ELLs among their students. Thus, they specify that these were not classrooms where the primary goal was to use content as a way to deliver language learning. Rather, in working with the content teachers, they were bringing a language-based perspective to a content classroom in order to help students better understand the content.

The project emphasized an understanding of how different language features contribute to the meaning that a speaker or writer is trying to convey. The researchers found that this approach allowed teachers who did not have a background in linguistics or language teaching to analyze—and to help their students analyze—the content of a text. For example, in working with history teachers, the focus was on recognizing 'what happened, who did it and to whom, and under what circumstances' by an analysis of the parts of the text that answer these questions.

Schleppegrell and her colleagues have used the systemic functional approach in providing professional development to a large number of teachers, most of whom work with ELLs in secondary schools in the USA. They have found that teachers reach a better understanding of the challenges students face in getting meaning from complex academic language and they come to recognize that students have difficulties in interpreting text, even if they have learned the vocabulary. In a review of work on teaching academic language to students at the secondary school level, Schleppegrell & O'Hallaron (2011) make this observation:

> Although many mainstream content-area teachers do not see themselves as language teachers, at the secondary level it is they who are likely to have the deepest content-area knowledge and who are therefore best positioned to support students' academic language development. … Teachers need strategies embedded in a rich curricular context in order to adequately address the complexities of language learning and teaching in secondary school subjects: vocabulary instruction, while necessary for academic language development, does not provide enough support for learning in the secondary content areas.
>
> (Schleppegrell & O'Hallaron, 2011, p. 14)

They suggest that systemic functional approaches to language analysis can help teachers develop these strategies. They urge further that scholars working in the area of applied linguistics need to engage in dialogue with teachers and with scholars in other areas of education so that more comprehensive approaches to teaching both language and content can be implemented.

The challenge of learning history in a developing L2 was also the focus of action research by Zwiers (2006). He reports on creating a chant based on ideas that he drew from his middle school ELL students about why it is important to study history. The chant was one of many activities that helped students become familiar with some of the important concepts and vocabulary that they would encounter in their history class. The chant concludes:

> Since books can be wrong and boring, too
> We look at primary source evidence.
> We evaluate it to help us understand
> different sides of the arguments.
>
> (Zwiers, 2006)

Because the chant was repeated often, it also contributed to students' fluency in using the terminology of their history discussions. Phrases such as 'primary source evidence' and 'understanding different sides of an argument' could be produced and understood automatically, contributing to their ability to engage in content-based discussions.

In some contexts, experiments in CBLT have been particularly difficult, and the local resources have not proved adequate to meet the expectations of all participants. For example, in Malaysia, a decision was made in 2003 to use CBLT to teach mathematics and science, with the dual goals of enhancing students' knowledge of English and maintaining a high standard in their academic knowledge of the two content subjects taught in that language. Tan (2011) carried out a study of how the English, mathematics, and science teachers understood their responsibilities and how their beliefs were reflected in their pedagogical practices.

In most classes, teachers who had been trained to teach mathematics and science were given some additional professional development for teaching these courses through English, and they were paired with English teachers who were meant to provide ongoing support for the content teachers as they gained experience. Tan found that teachers tended to see themselves as *either* content teachers *or* English teachers. Furthermore, Tan reports that even though students at the secondary school level received some academic support through English for Science and Technology courses, the content of these courses was not coordinated with the mathematics and science classes that the students were being taught in English by other teachers.

Tan & Lan (2011) report that there were substantial differences between the level of English that could successfully be used in urban and non-urban schools. As end-of-year examinations approached, teachers were concerned about whether students understood the content and sometimes used translation to the students' L1 to try to make sure that happened. Tan & Lan found that such practices helped comprehension at the moment, but did not help students develop speaking and writing abilities in English. The practice was also found to make it difficult for some students to perform well on examinations that were administered in English.

> Although [mathematics and science teachers] address content comprehension in their lessons, they have not considered what linguistic support students as ELLs need in order learn [English for academic purposes]. This is especially true in terms of oral and written production. Their unproblematic assumption that student comprehension in [their L1] will automatically transfer into performance in the exam context contradicts what students themselves say they can do.
>
> (Tan & Lan, 2011, p. 17)

Malaysia, like other countries in the Asia-Pacific region, has an education system that is highly exam-driven and which strives for outstanding performance in fields such as science and mathematics. In 2009, the Minister of Education announced that the policy of teaching mathematics and science in English was being reversed (Gooch, 2009). Some observers saw the decision as being mainly political, but the government's position was that students' performance on mathematics and science examinations had declined since the policy was implemented and that students did not appear to be learning these important academic subjects in English as well as they had in Bahasa Malaysia, their L1. The issue remains controversial, and it is certainly the case that the brief experiment may be said to have ended before some of the types of professional development and curriculum reform that might have succeeded had time to work. For now, however, the government's policy is to return to teaching English as a subject and to end the practice of using is as a medium for teaching mathematics and science.

Learning challenging academic content in a new language at the secondary school level is difficult for students in all types of CBLT environments. It may be particularly difficult for students from minority-language backgrounds, whose instruction is entirely in L2, especially those who cannot build on prior academic experience in their L1. Students depend on instruction that is adapted to their needs, but the adaptations should seek to make age-appropriate content accessible to them by the use of pedagogical strategies that help them understand the content rather than by simplifying it.

Kinsella (1997) acknowledges the value of adapted materials and sheltered instruction, including the variety of interactive classroom activities that have been shown to engage learners in positive learning experiences. However, she warns about the kind of dependency that can be created if students who are overwhelmed by the challenges of mainstream instruction 'simply wait for the ESL or sheltered content teacher to skillfully identify and explain the main points' (p. 51). She provides practical guidelines for preparing students to learn in the more traditional mainstream settings by teaching them learning strategies that can help them cope with the challenges. She says that

> ... any student who aspires to genuine secondary school success and an eventual college degree or training for a technological field must have a repertoire of effective strategies for learning within traditional formats (such as lectures) as well as within more progressive formats (such as cooperative structures) ... Motivated second language learners may consequently emerge from the week's sheltered biology unit with a deeper understanding of human anatomy and an appreciation for learning with and from peers; however, they may be no better equipped to tackle the next textbook chapter on their own, take effective lecture notes, prepare for an upcoming exam, expand their academic English vocabulary, or competently answer an essay question.
>
> (Kinsella, 1997, p. 52)

Kinsella proposes a detailed approach to helping learners understand what they must do in order to become independent 'active learners', including a range of strategies from learning how to read a textbook chapter and developing effective vocabulary learning tools to using the correct language formulas so that, in mainstream classes, they will know how to interrupt, ask for clarification, and request assistance from the teacher. Such training in learning strategies falls within Nation's language-focused learning strand and is intended to prepare students to move beyond the limitations of adapted instruction and put them on a path to success in education.

Learning the Language in CBLT

For adolescents who are beginning to learn a second language or who are using the L2 in a content-learning environment for the first time, age can entail both advantages and disadvantages. The advantages include cognitive maturity and an awareness of what their goals and challenges are. The greatest advantages are present for more mature students who have developed strong L1 literacy skills and content knowledge through studies in their L1. For these students, knowledge of how language works, how spoken and written language differ, as well as the experience of what it means to be a student, can provide an excellent basis for going on to learn an L2 and to use that new language to continue learning academic content. For students whose L1 and L2 have a shared origin, there will also be advantages for vocabulary and grammar learning as students recognize similarities between the languages.

Adolescent students who have not developed literacy in L1 or whose schooling has been interrupted may come to school with a strong motivation to benefit from the opportunity to learn both the L2 and academic content, but, for them, age can represent some disadvantages, most significantly, the gap between their academic content knowledge and language skill and that of their peers who have benefited from years of education through the language of instruction. Those disadvantages can be overcome in a learning environment where they are given adequate support and time for learning.

Unlike young children, minority-language students who enter a CBLT program at the secondary school level cannot depend on imitating their peers as a basis for learning the language that is necessary to meet their academic needs. Simply doing what other students do and saying what they say will allow them to participate in some social interactions, but the linguistic demands of academic learning at this level require them to use language independently in doing tasks and assignments at school and at home, and it takes time for them to acquire the language skills they need.

The learner's age is a consideration for majority-language students in immersion and CLIL programs as well. Majority-language students who continue their study of the second or foreign language they started learning in CBLT programs in primary school have a good chance of developing a level of proficiency that will allow them to travel for work or study in places where their L2 is spoken. If they do not continue their L2 studies in secondary school, the investment they have made during the elementary school years may not yield the long term language proficiency they had hoped for. Spotlight Study 4.1 shows how French immersion students' language abilities are related to their experiences in secondary school.

Spotlight Study 4.1

Turnbull, Lapkin, Hart, & Swain (1998) looked at the French proficiency of Grade 12 English L1 students who had participated in French immersion programs in several Canadian regions where French is not widely spoken in the community. They compared the results for students who started French immersion in kindergarten or Grade 1 (EI—early immersion), in Grade 5 (MI—middle immersion), or Grade 7 (LI—late immersion). Their research addressed two of the most frequently asked questions in the language learning literature:

1 Is time on task the best predictor of long-term success?
2 Are the best results obtained if L2 learning begins when students are very young?

Table 4.1 summarizes several important aspects of the students' exposure to French at school.

	EI	MI	LI
Starting grade for immersion	K–1	5	7
Total hours French instruction through Grade 8 [a]	5670	2040	1260
Total hours CBLT (Immersion) through Grade 8	5670	1800	900
Median number hours French instruction in Grades 9–12	1440	960	1440
Total instruction in French at school [b]	7110	3000	2700

a The data in the original table have been simplified by rounding or averaging.
b The hours spent in non-immersion French instruction were in 'core French' classes.

Table 4.1 Turnbull et al. (1998) Study of French language outcomes in different immersion programs

Table 4.1 shows that the students who began their French immersion experience when they were in kindergarten or Grade 1 accumulated more than twice as many hours of instruction as those in middle immersion and late immersion. The difference in the number of hours might lead to the prediction that students with the greatest number of hours of instruction would perform best. The belief that it is always better for L2 learning to begin as early as possible would also support that prediction.

At first glance, the results of this study support the predictions. EI students performed better than both the MI and LI students on speaking ability, measured in terms of accuracy in a sentence repetition task, and there were no differences between the MI and LI students. However, on most other measures, including a cloze test, a reading comprehension test, and both written and oral 'opinion' measures, there were no significant differences across the groups. That is, although EI students had spent twice as much time learning, their French proficiency was not consistently better than that of the students who had started French immersion later. ■

What does this study suggest about the relative benefits of an early start? On the one hand, the findings confirm that students who begin learning later may benefit from their cognitive maturity and their L1 literacy skills, allowing them to learn L2 more quickly than students who begin learning earlier. The authors are quick to caution, however, that this study cannot be used as a basis for concluding that late immersion should replace early immersion. Let's look at some other findings from the study and at some of the characteristics of the learners that may have contributed to the authors' cautionary comments.

One of the most striking findings of this study is that, for EI and MI students, higher levels of French language performance measured at the end of Grade 12 were correlated with the number of courses in French that students chose to take *at the secondary level*. These positive correlations were present, not only on measures of reading and writing skill, which one might expect to be strengthened by studies at the secondary level, but also on measures of speaking and listening. This correlation was not seen in the LI group, perhaps because most of the LI students had taken a large number of courses in French throughout their secondary schooling, making it difficult to include students with a low number of courses in the analysis. The authors acknowledge that this finding might reflect an effect of 'recency' as well as proficiency. That is, most of the LI students were still substantially immersed in their French instruction, while there was greater variation in the 'recent' experience of the other groups, some of whom had discontinued French language studies.

Other possible reasons for the lack of a straightforward positive correlation between the total amount of time spent in learning French and the outcomes at the end of secondary school include the self-selecting nature of the LI. That is, there is some evidence that the range of overall abilities among the younger students was greater than among the older students. It is quite possible that students with higher academic ability and motivation would choose to participate in the challenging LI programs and that students experiencing difficulty probably had more control over the number of hours they devoted to French studies at the secondary level. Thus, one implication of the study may be that students with a great variety of abilities can succeed in EI programs, while LI programs fit the needs of students with stronger motivation and academic abilities. For all students, however, there appears to have been a benefit to continuing to participate in the CBLT program in the later years of secondary school.

Another study that sheds light on the relationship between time and language learning comes from research by Lasagabaster (2008) in the Basque Country in Spain. In that context, students are taught in Spanish and Basque throughout their education, and when they begin to study English or French, they are learning a third language. Fitting three languages into a school schedule is a challenge, and Lasagabaster emphasizes that many educators believe that CLIL 'is the best way to improve students' command of foreign languages *without devoting too much time to their teaching*' (p. 30) [emphasis added].

Lasagabaster examined the performance of students in their third and fourth years of secondary school (age 14–16) on a variety of tests of oral and written English. All students had begun learning English as a school subject at the age of eight and all continued to receive three hours per week of instruction in English as a foreign language. In addition, two of the three groups had also had either one or two years of CLIL instruction, adding four hours per week of exposure to English in an environment where the language was rarely heard or used outside the English class. On every measure of language proficiency, the CLIL students performed significantly better than the non-CLIL students, and on some measures, their performance was dramatically better. Lasagabaster acknowledges that 'students who chose the demanding CLIL programmes may have been more academically gifted and more motivated than their non-CLIL counterparts' (p. 38). However, another intriguing finding of this study is that, in contrast to much research on educational achievement, the level of parental education was not a strong predictor of students' acquisition of English in CLIL programs. This appears to add strength to the hypothesis that CLIL is an effective program for students with a variety of backgrounds and abilities.

Research carried out in the European Schools gives further insight into how time on task and age are related to the development of L2 skills, and adds the dimension of a wider learning context to the analysis. In Chapter 3 we saw that the development of language proficiency by young students in the European Schools is associated with the status and availability of the L2 in the larger community. A study of students from Grade 5 to the end of the secondary level shows that this contextual difference remains important. That is, students who studied English in a school located in England were more proficient in English than those who had received their education in schools located in other European countries (Housen, 2002a, b) even though they continued to experience the same instructional and curricular program within the school environment. More striking, however, is the progress made by students in the European Schools that are located in countries where English is not the community language. By the end of secondary school, students in all the learning contexts had reached very high levels of performance such that the out-of-school context was no longer associated with a substantial difference between groups. Housen points to two factors in this eventual convergence: the overall amount of time students spent in learning their L2 and the inclusion of both content-based and language-based instruction in the students' program.

In addition, a study of Dutch, French, and Greek students learning English from Grade 5 to the end of the secondary level suggests that the linguistic 'distance' between students' L1 and L2 also has an important role (Ringbom & Jarvis, 2009). Dutch students acquired English vocabulary quickly in the early years, suggesting an advantage due to the large number of cognates in the basic vocabulary of the two languages. By the end of secondary school, however, differences between groups were much smaller, and no longer significant. At first glance, this might appear to reflect the benefits of Greco-Latin cognates at more advanced vocabulary levels. However, as Housen (2002a) points out, the lexical richness measure was based on students' telling of a picture story and drew primarily on non-academic vocabulary. These findings suggest that students from both groups had acquired comparable ability to use English for narrative tasks.

Housen et al. (2011) studied the English language development of German students between the ages of 10 and 14 in regular English as a foreign language (EFL) instruction, in English medium instruction in European Schools in Germany and Belgium, and in European Schools instruction in England. The findings of this study were consistent with those in their earlier study that learning English where it is the language of the wider community led to greater proficiency in the language. However, the researchers were surprised to find that students in the regular EFL group performed as well as and indeed often better than those in the European Schools located in Germany and Belgium. They offered several explanations for this, including the possibility that because the regular foreign language students were older, their cognitive maturity and educational experience made them better test-takers.

It is noteworthy that the findings of the Housen et al. study are also compatible with a factor that runs through their studies with students at the elementary and secondary levels. The researchers have observed that the approach to second language teaching in European Schools emphasizes communicative interaction and comprehension at the primary school level but that when students reach the secondary school, they not only receive more content-based instruction but also more explicit language-focused instruction. Housen and his colleagues suggest that the language-focused instruction makes important contributions to students' metalinguistic knowledge that would be especially useful on measures such as the cloze test used in their research.

Vocabulary Learning

The importance of vocabulary learning for students in CBLT programs has been underlined many times. The challenge of learning and using the academic vocabulary at the secondary school level can seem overwhelming. Reading has been cited as an essential way of building vocabulary, but as we saw in Chapter 3 in the discussion of research by Gardner (2004, 2008), students must read a great deal and they must read many different kinds of texts if they are to encounter the range of vocabulary they need for academic studies.

Students certainly benefit from opportunities for incidental vocabulary learning through reading. However, research has made it clear that learners also benefit from direct instruction to expand their vocabulary to the level needed for more advanced academic work (Beck et al., 2002; Benjamin & Crow, 2010; Nation, 2001). Furthermore, learning vocabulary through reading can be particularly difficult in some subject matters. Met (2008) points out how mathematics texts, for example, can be misleading. Even so-called 'story problems' do not necessarily present good vocabulary learning opportunities.

> It is usually not possible to guess the meanings of words from context, and skipping unknown words in the hope that their meanings will be clarified later rarely works. Often, the text is too short to provide the necessary multiple encounters that allow for contextual guessing to be successful. Further, story problems tend to be parsimonious, with few of the natural redundancies found in narrative texts. Decoding skills

> can also be problematic since symbols used in texts are not amenable to decoding. Reading strategies that are useful in constructing meaning from narrative text may not be applicable to story problems ... Specific vocabulary (for example, quotient, denominator), frequent use of abbreviations (in., cm.), as well as the way in which language is used in mathematics ('Let *x* =') are not common to social interaction or other kinds of text and may be confusing to L2 learners.
>
> (Met, 2008, p. 53)

In an analysis of classroom discourse in CLIL instruction, Dalton-Puffer (2007) found that most of the errors students made were in vocabulary. Vocabulary was also the aspect of students' language that teachers were most likely to respond to with corrective feedback. Dalton-Puffer points to two possible reasons for this finding. First, the language produced by students was usually limited to fairly brief utterances—a few words or a simple sentence—making errors in grammar less likely to occur. This has also been reported in other CBLT contexts and indeed in much classroom interaction, where it is the teacher who is most likely to produce long presentations and explanations while students typically respond briefly to questions rather than producing multi-sentence monologues. In French immersion the lack of sustained student output has been a matter of concern for a long time (for example, Allen, Fröhlich, & Spada, 1984; Swain & Carroll, 1987). In developing effective pedagogy for CBLT, teachers have looked for ways to increase students' opportunities to produce meaning-focused output, for example by asking questions that require longer and more thoughtful answers (Echevarria & Graves, 2007) and through various types of collaborative work (Swain & Lapkin, 2001). We will return to this topic when we discuss group-work in language learning.

According to Dalton-Puffer (2007), another reason that vocabulary errors are far more frequent than any other kind is that 'the context of the content subject stretches students' lexical abilities to an extent where they a) exhibit frequent lexical gaps and b) make explicit attempts at filling them' (p. 281). Dalton-Puffer contrasts this to typical foreign language instruction, where the topics for oral interaction are often limited in scope, making it less likely that students will encounter large numbers of new words unless the teacher explicitly introduces them into the classroom activity. We saw this illustrated in Classroom Snapshot 4.1.

Majority-language students in foreign language immersion and CLIL programs typically have the advantage of acquiring considerable academic vocabulary in their L1. For minority-language students whose L1 vocabulary has not been developed through academic study, the acquisition of L2 vocabulary entails the additional challenge of learning the new concepts as well as the language to name or describe them. While it is true that using academic language requires much more than vocabulary, there is no doubt that without adequate vocabulary development, students' progress will often be blocked.

Corrective Feedback and Language-Focused Learning

As we have seen, feedback has been identified as an important feature of language acquisition, either because it confirms that communication has been successful or because it informs the learner that there is a lack of clarity or an error in what was said or written. Research with students between the ages of 12 and 18 has included descriptive investigations of the feedback students get in CBLT classrooms and some experimental studies comparing different feedback types.

In experimental studies, research has confirmed the benefits of feedback that is provided during content-based lessons, with a focus on features other than vocabulary alone. The feedback is most effective if it is sufficiently explicit so that students are able to shift their attention briefly to the language itself before returning their attention to the academic content. Classroom Snapshot 4.4 comes from one of the first of these experimental studies.

Classroom Snapshot 4.4

Students in a middle school science class (Grades 6, 7, and 8) are learning to present science reports on experiments or observations they have carried out. Most of the students have Spanish as their first language, but there are a few students from other first languages as well. The presentation of a science experiment typically includes both a report of what was found and a statement of the prediction or hypothesis that the student had before completing the experiment or observation.

José: I think that the worm will go under the soil.
Teacher: I *think* that the worm *will* go under the soil?
José: [no response]
Teacher: I *thought* that the worm *would* go under the soil.
José: I *thought* that the worm *would* go under the soil.

(Doughty & Varela, 1998, p. 124)

Spotlight Study 4.2

Classroom Snapshot 4.4 is taken from Doughty & Varela's (1998) study of the effect of providing feedback to ELL students in US schools as they worked on their science projects. Student participants in this project were 11–14 years old and grouped by their English proficiency rather than by grade level. Each of the two classes had students from Grades 6, 7, and 8. Each class had a different teacher, but they were following the same science program. Both teachers acknowledged that their focus was almost exclusively on the science content and that they very rarely focused on any aspect of grammar, either through explicit instruction or feedback on error. Students received some grammar instruction in their language arts classes, but even there, the emphasis was on communicative skills. Students had a wide range of English abilities, but most continued to be 'nontargetlike in their use of many features of English' (p. 119). This lack of proficiency in English was seen as possibly preventing the students from doing well when they were integrated into mainstream classes, which, for most, would happen in the following year.

For this study, the two teachers agreed to teach the same science program over a period of several weeks, with one teacher proceeding as she always had done—without special attention to any language feature. The other teacher was to offer the students feedback on their use of simple past tense verbs (for example, 'The worm *went* under the soil') and past conditionals (for example, 'I predicted that the worm *would go* under the soil.'). The feedback was provided on both oral and written uses of the verbs in the students' science reports. Classroom Snapshot 4.4 shows a typical exchange between a student and the teacher using this technique: When a student made an error in using the simple past or conditional verbs, the teacher would repeat the students' sentence, with emphasis on the word that needed attention. If the student did not respond to this indication that an error was being signaled, the teacher then provided the correct form as a recast.

The teacher used the corrective recast technique as students were working on their reports but not when they were presenting in front of the class. In the latter case, she provided feedback in a discussion of a video recording of the presentation. In these interactions with the whole class, students discussed the strengths of each report and ways it could have been better. In addition, the teacher paused the video to point out errors in the past tense and asked students to repeat the correct form all together. The teacher in this study provided a similar type of feedback on students' written reports, circling the error and providing the correct form.

Doughty and Varela used a pre-test to determine how students used past tense verb forms before the feedback intervention and a post-test to assess their use of the past tense verbs after the intervention. They also administered a delayed post-test two months after the intervention had ended.

On the post-test, the group that had received corrective feedback performed significantly better on every measure of verb use than they had on the pre-test. A similar pattern was observed on the delayed post-test. Perhaps even more striking is the fact that the comparison group, who had continued to carry out the same science activities and prepared the same types of oral and written reports showed no change in their use of these verb forms over the period. In fact, whereas the comparison group had, on average, done better with these verbs on the pre-test, the feedback group outperformed them on all the post-test and delayed post-test measures of verb use.

One important aspect of this research was that students' progress was measured not only in terms of how many verbs they used correctly, but also in terms of changes in the types of errors they made. The researcher and the teacher were interested in evidence that some change had taken place in the students' understanding of the verbs that were to be used in the science reports, whether or not that change led them to use the verbs without any errors. Thus, a distinction was made between 'nontargetlike' uses (for example, 'I think the worm *go* under ...') and 'interlanguage' uses (for example, 'I think the worm *wode* go under ...'). Students who received the corrective feedback were more likely to produce fewer non-targetlike and more target-like and interlanguage forms. ■

The Doughty & Varela research described in Spotlight Study 4.2 leads to several inferences. First, content teachers can identify features of their students' language use that are important for a particular task or type of activity. Such language features may be either those that Snow, Met, & Genesee identified as content-obligatory or content-compatible. In the case of the science experiments, the obligatory language would include the vocabulary for the different elements of the experiment. Arguably, the use of simple past tense and past conditional verb forms is also content-obligatory if the science reports were to make clear the students' hypotheses, their actions, and their results. The accuracy of the verb forms, including their accurate spelling, while desirable, would not be necessary for showing that the student had completed the experiment and understood its results. Thus, a science teacher might choose to emphasize the vocabulary and the marking of verbs for simple past and past conditional during the science class, making accurate spelling the focus in a separate language-focused activity.

Another inference that can be drawn from the Doughty and Varela study is that when teachers choose to focus on a limited number of important language elements *during* content-based lessons, students can improve their language performance. The findings of this study may be seen as contrasting with other studies, for example, the Lyster & Ranta (1997) study discussed earlier. They found that students rarely responded to a teacher's feedback when it was in the form of a recast. However, it is important to note that, in the Doughty and Varela study, the teacher's recasts were targeted to a very limited number of language features and that the type of recast included clear indications of what error the teacher was responding to.

Thus, a third inference from this study is that recasts are likely to be most effective in a meaning-focused lesson or activity if teachers indicate clearly what they want students to notice in the feedback. In this case, the teacher repeated the error (or, in the written work, circled it), and then provided the correct form. In the oral feedback, the teacher used stress and intonation to emphasize what it was she wanted students to pay attention to.

Finally, the teacher who provided the corrective recasts also encouraged students to repeat the correct form. Such repetition is, to be sure, not an indication that the student has internalized the correction. However, it is another way of ensuring that the student has recognized what the focus of the feedback is. It also gives the student an opportunity to practice, within a transfer-appropriate context, language forms that are similar to those they will need when they report on another science experiment.

Group-Work in Language Learning

As noted above, students in CBLT classes—as in many instructional settings—do not typically have many opportunities to participate in extended discourse. They are more likely to respond to teachers' questions in short sentences or single words. One way of increasing meaning-focused output is through the use of cooperative or collaborative activities carried out in groups. We have seen the effectiveness of this for students in content-based activities. Some activities can also be useful in helping students to focus on language itself, combining opportunities for meaning-focused and language-focused learning.

Two classroom activities that encourage students to focus on language as they produce comprehensible output are story construction and dictogloss (Swain & Lapkin, 1998, 2002; Wajnryb, 1990). Both activities are often done by students working in pairs or small groups. In story construction, students are shown a series of pictures and told to produce a story that the pictures illustrate. In the dictogloss activity, students hear a text read aloud at a speed that does not allow them to write it directly from dictation. They must, instead, listen for content and then reconstruct the text, usually by working with a partner. Kowal & Swain (1997) observed English-speaking students in French immersion classes engaged in both these activities. The resulting *collaborative dialogues* show how students try to find the right words and the right sentence patterns to achieve their goal. In these conversations, students may sometimes use English, but their primary focus is on the language they need to complete the task.

Classroom Snapshot 4.5 is an excerpt from a collaborative dialogue between students in Grade 8 working on a dictogloss text. The sentence they have remembered and are trying to reconstruct includes the phrase *les problèmes qui nous tracassent* [the problems that trouble us]. They are trying to figure out what the subject of the verb is so that they can find the verb form that agrees with the subject. They are distracted by the object pronoun *nous* that precedes the verb in French and which they briefly mistake for the subject of the verb. They finally get some help from the teacher.

Classroom Snapshot 4.5

After several turns in which the students search in a verb reference book for the correct conjugation of *tracasser*, they continue trying to solve the problem. Note that the verb form they need to write is the third person plural *tracassent* which is pronounced exactly like the first and third person singular *tracasse* and second person singular *tracasses*. The students' interaction is mostly in French, and an English version is shown in square brackets.

George: *Les problèmes qui nous tracassent.* Like the … *c'est les problèmes …* like, that concern us. [The problems that trouble us. Like the … it's the problems … like, that concern us.]

Keith: *Oui, mais 'tracasse' n'est-ce pas que c'est o–n–s?* [Yes, but 'tracasse' isn't it o–n–s? (Keith is proposing that they need the ending that goes with *nous*.)]

George: *Tracasse c'est pas un, c'est pas un … oui,* I dunno. ['Tracasse' is not a, is not a … yes, I dunno.]

Keith: *OK, ça dit, les problèmes qui nous tracassent. Donc, est-ce que 'tracasse' est un verbe? Qu'on, qu'on doit conjuger?* [Okay, it says, 'the problems that trouble us.' So, is *tracasse* a verb? That we have to conjugate? (asking the teacher)]

Teacher: Uh, huh.

Keith: *Donc, est-ce que c'est tracassons?* [So, is it *tracassons*?]

Teacher: *Ce sont les 'problèmes' qui nous tracassent.* [It's the 'problems' that trouble us.]

George: *Nous, c'est, c'est pas, c'est pas, oui*, c'est les problèmes, c'est pas, c'est pas 'nous'.* [We, it's, it's not, it's not, yes* (understanding that *les problèmes* is the subject) it's the 'problems', it's not 'we'.]

Keith: *Ah! e-n-t* [the correct ending]. *OK, OK.*

Note: It seems likely that in this case it is the English word 'we' rather than the French word oui (yes) that was intended. ■

The students in Classroom Snapshot 4.5 eventually work out the correct answer. The verb ending they need is *–ent*. They do not use much metalinguistic terminology except to ask whether *tracasse* is a verb that they need to conjugate, but they work out that *les problèmes* and not *nous* is the subject of the sentence. And then, with the teacher's help, they realize what they need to do.

In completing tasks such as this, students may discuss many aspects of the passage. When their attention is on the language itself and how to write the text correctly, the interaction is referred to as **a language-related episode** (LRE). In studies that have analyzed students' work in pairs and groups in terms of the LREs that occur, researchers have found that learners' language knowledge and use can be affected in positive ways by this experience. On tests that specifically measure students' knowledge of the language forms they focus on in their LREs, it is evident that they often recall the solution they reached—whether it was the correct one or not (Swain & Lapkin, 2001). Such findings highlight the importance of ensuring, as Gibbons (2002) suggests (see Chapter 2, page 47), that the tasks assigned for pair- and group-work are within the students' abilities, that they know what the end-point is, and that they have the resources to complete the tasks in the time available.

In these collaborative activities, students engage in both meaning-focused interaction and language-focused learning. These activities allow them to collaborate both on using language to understand and express meaning and on learning new language or retrieving the language they know but do not always use correctly to express meaning accurately and appropriately.

Summary

Success in understanding academic content is no guarantee that students' L2 proficiency will continue to develop toward greater accuracy, sophistication, and appropriate use. Adolescents who are learning L2 in CBLT contexts need explicit language-focused instruction and feedback as well as continuing opportunities to use language in a wide variety of social and academic contexts if their proficiency is to reach levels appropriate to their age.

It takes several years for students to achieve age-appropriate knowledge and skill in their L2. Even students who begin learning L2 at the elementary school level are likely to have much still to learn when they reach the secondary school. Adolescents need time to continue learning the language for academic purposes, even after they have acquired the socially appropriate language for interaction with their peers. When students begin learning L2 at the secondary school level, the linguistic demands they face are considerable—both in the social sphere and the academic environment.

The challenge is great for students in all types of CBLT programs, but it may be greatest for minority-language students. If their L1 education has been interrupted or incomplete, they will face the additional challenge of learning 'how to learn' in school. If they have had previous L1 education, their prior knowledge, cognitive maturity, and metalinguistic ability may help them learn more quickly than younger students, but this more rapid learning does not ensure that their language abilities will continue to develop without language-focused instruction. Whatever their background and previous learning experience, students need continuing support for language development and academic content learning over a period of years, and the secondary school years are of crucial importance.

5 CBLT: What We Know Now

Preview

In this chapter, we will return to the statements about CBLT that you responded to in Activity 1.1. For each statement, I will provide a response based on the research that has been reviewed in this book. Before you read my responses, review your own ideas by returning to your responses in Activity 1.1.

Activity 5.1: Review your opinions
In Activity 1.1 (page 7), you indicated how strongly you agreed with some statements about Content Based Language Teaching. Before you continue reading this chapter, go back and complete the questionnaire again. Compare the responses you gave then to those you would give now. Have your views about CBLT been changed or confirmed by what you've read in the preceding chapters?

Reflecting on Ideas about CBLT: Learning from Research

1 In CBLT, if students understand the academic content, language learning will take care of itself.

Understanding what we hear or read is an essential first step in acquiring a new language. If learners have access to comprehensible meaning-focused input, they will eventually internalize some of the words and patterns that they hear most frequently or those that they find most interesting. However, after decades of research on language acquisition in CBLT in a variety of educational and social contexts, it is clear that language acquisition does not 'take care of itself.'

Students can spend years in classes where they understand the content and even do well on tests of that content, in both their L1 and their L2, and yet continue to make grammatical errors, use a limited vocabulary, and miss important cues regarding the appropriateness of certain language features. As Lyster (2011) remarks, 'contrary to the "two for one" nomenclature, nothing comes for free. ... a great deal of attention still needs to be drawn to the second language, which needs to be manipulated and enhanced during content teaching' (Lyster 2011, p. 612).

To get the most out of their CBLT experience, students need opportunities to focus on both content and language—sometimes in ways that integrate the two, sometimes in ways that direct their attention to one or the other for a period of time. Learning a second or foreign language to a high degree of proficiency takes time, but it can be facilitated by focused attention to language. One useful framework for thinking about what students need as they learn language and content is Nation's Four Strands, with three out of four strands devoted to activities that are meaning-focused and a crucial fourth strand in which the challenges of learning the language itself can be in focus.

2 *It is not appropriate for teachers to correct students' language errors during content-based lessons.*

Many teachers express reluctance to respond to language errors while students' attention is on academic content. They prefer to leave such language-focused learning to a separate lesson or even to another teacher. It is true that language-focused instruction that is separate from ongoing meaning-focused activity has a place in language learning, but separation of meaning-focused and language-focused learning does not mean that they are unrelated to each other. During language-focused lessons students should learn language features that will be useful when they are engaged in meaning-focused academic content lessons.

In addition to providing some specifically language-focused lessons and activities however, teachers can help students by providing feedback on language errors during meaning-focused activities in content-based lessons. Learning something in the context where they will need to use it and while using the cognitive processes that are typical of academic work encourages transfer-appropriate processing and the greater likelihood that what is learned in this context will be remembered in similar ones.

In providing feedback on language during content lessons, teachers need to make sure that students know when the feedback applies to the language rather than the content. Furthermore, the feedback should target a limited number of language features, especially features that are content-obligatory or content-compatible.

Teachers must always exercise their judgment about whether corrective feedback is likely to distract students from the content in a content-based lesson. Responding to every error or stopping the interaction to explain a language rule at length would be inconsistent with good pedagogy in a CBLT class.

3 Second language learners in CBLT should use the same instructional materials as students who are already proficient in the language of instruction.

When students begin learning academic content in a second language, they need considerable support if they are to make effective use of materials written for proficient users of that language. Thus, it is important to provide instructional materials that take account of their limitations as their linguistic knowledge and skills develop. Trying to understand spoken and written input that is too far beyond their current language level can lead to frustration, loss of motivation, and even a withdrawal from the learning context.

Thus, there is an important place for simplified or modified materials in the CBLT classroom. L2 learners can gain substantial benefit from materials that are at a level of linguistic difficulty that allows them to understand what they hear or read with a low or moderate degree of difficulty. For example, in sheltered content instruction, students can begin to engage with the academic content that is appropriate to their age level before they have acquired the linguistic competence that is needed for the materials that are designed for L1 speakers of the same age.

However, for most students, the goal of CBLT is to develop beyond the beginner level and to gain independence in using the new language. Most minority-language students hope to achieve a level of skill that will allow them to be integrated into mainstream classrooms; majority-language students may wish to travel abroad for work or study. Thus, they also need experience in interacting with the authentic academic material appropriate to their age, and they need the teacher's help in acquiring strategies for gaining access to this material, even when their language skills are still developing (Kinsella, 1997).

4 It is best to begin CBLT after students have developed good reading skills in their L1.

Research with English language learners has confirmed the benefits of either teaching reading in L1 first or teaching L1 and L2 reading at the same time. Not only does such an approach allow students to capitalize on vocabulary and language patterns that they already understand, it has also been shown in many cases to enhance students' eventual proficiency in L2 (Goldenberg, 2008).

CBLT programs for majority-language students vary in how they sequence L1 and L2 reading. In North American immersion programs that begin when students are in kindergarten, many studies have reported positive results for introducing reading in the L2 first. Some researchers have suggested that, because students have so little opportunity to hear or use the language outside the classroom, maximizing its use from the very beginning can lead to better L2 outcomes at no cost to long-term L1 retention and development, which remains a priority in their education. In these North American contexts, students show early lags in their English reading, but they quickly catch up with their English-educated peers when they begin to have reading instruction in English at about Grade 3.

In immersion programs in China and elsewhere in Asia, as well as in the CLIL and European Schools programs, students usually receive their first reading instruction in their L1, and that language is the primary language for content examinations throughout their primary schooling (Housen, 2002a,b). What seems most valuable in all contexts is to ensure that students are encouraged to develop literacy in both languages, whether simultaneously or sequentially.

5 Students in CBLT need to have grammar and vocabulary instruction that is separate from content-based lessons.

The first part of this statement has been confirmed time and again: Students in CBLT need to have grammar and vocabulary instruction. Without it, they may continue making the same grammatical errors, using vocabulary that is less than precise, or continuing to use ways of speaking that are not entirely appropriate. Language-focused learning has been shown to improve outcomes in language proficiency in a variety of CBLT classrooms. The question of whether this language-focused learning should be provided in separate lessons needs to be explored further (Harley, 1998; Lyster, 2007).

As we saw in the discussion of statement 2 above, there are advantages to helping students focus on particular language features in lessons that do not require them to also try to learn academic content at the same time. However, classroom-based research suggests that separate language-focused lessons are most valuable if they are coordinated with the meaning-focused content-based lessons. That is, what students learn in any grammar and vocabulary instruction should be of use to them when they return to a focus on the academic content (Nation, 2007).

6 Teachers often fail to distinguish between a student's language abilities and subject matter knowledge.

There is some evidence that this is true in many CBLT situations, especially those in which L2 learners have opportunities to interact with peers who speak the language as their L1. Students acquire the ability to use the L2 for social interaction and may appear quite proficient in those settings (Cummins, 2000). However, the acquisition of the kind of language that is needed to understand and express academic content information has been found to take much longer. This can lead to teachers assuming that a student's academic difficulties are due to a lack of effort or motivation or to cognitive limitations, leading to incorrect placement of students in classes that are designed for students who have developmental or learning disabilities, or behavior problems. Such errors of placement can deprive students of opportunities to continue developing their academic language abilities.

Teachers and parents may also err in the opposite direction. When L2 students are struggling in school, it may be assumed that they simply haven't yet developed the necessary language proficiency for the academic work when in fact they need specialized attention to help them overcome challenges such as specific language impairment or learning disabilities that would affect their success in L1. An added complication here is that it is often difficult to discover the underlying causes of students' problems if the school environment does not have professionals who speak the students' L1. It is essential for educators to look for evidence of students' abilities in a variety of modes, not just on the standard academic measures in the majority language. With experience, many teachers develop the ability to distinguish between difficulties that will work themselves out over time and those that require remediation or intervention of a more specialized kind, but educational systems and institutions need to develop better tools to help them evaluate students' difficulties (Fortune, 2010).

7 Students with learning or speech and language disabilities will have more difficulty in CBLT than they would in L1 instruction.

The research on this topic confirms that, when children have disabilities that are manifested in their L1, they are likely to have the same disabilities in their L2. In programs for majority-language students, there is sometimes pressure for students with special needs to leave the L2 learning context and return to L1 studies. However, research has shown that, with appropriate support—ideally in both L1 and L2—most students with speech and language disabilities, as well as those with developmental disabilities, can enjoy the benefits of learning a second language and also fulfill their potential for academic content learning (Fortune, 2010; Genesee, 1987). That is, although learning an additional language represents a challenge for students with these special needs, they can succeed in school. It is clear that minority-language students rarely have the choice of leaving L2 CBLT and continuing their studies in L1. For these students, L2 learning and achieving their potential in academic learning are essential. Educational institutions have a responsibility to develop programs and provide services to meet their needs.

8 CBLT is effective mainly because it allows students to spend more time using their L2.

The amount of time available for learning is one of the best predictors of outcomes in language development. In foreign-language settings, students whose contact with the L2 is limited to a few hours a week will find it very difficult to achieve high levels of proficiency, and more time for learning is certainly beneficial. However, increased time is no guarantee of success, nor is it the only reason for the success of CBLT.

Other benefits of CBLT include the motivational effect of using the language for genuine communicative interaction, focusing on topics that are of importance to a student's education in a greater variety of pedagogical activities, for example, group-work and project-based learning. CBLT also typically leads students to come in contact with a substantially larger vocabulary and range of language patterns and registers than is the case in regular foreign language instruction. Furthermore, a pedagogical approach that gives attention to both meaning-focused and language-focused learning, as well as the student's own desire to achieve high levels of proficiency make essential contributions to the success of CBLT (Lightbown & Spada, 2013).

Before leaving the topic of time, it is essential to say, again, that time spent in L1 development has been found, in the long run, to enhance L2 development. Language learning is not a zero-sum game in which improvement in one language must entail a loss of proficiency in the other. The goal of CBLT is additive bilingualism.

9 In CBLT, teachers should sometimes use the students' L1.

As suggested in the discussion of statement 8 above, the 'commonsense' notion that L1 should be banished from the L2 classroom does not take account of the many positive ways that L1 can contribute to students' further development. Learning a new language requires that learners spend time in meaning-focused activities that push them to try to understand and produce the new language. For that reason, it is best for teachers to use the L2 consistently and to use a variety of strategies to aid comprehension. Teachers should avoid 'running translations' that can teach students to wait for the 'easier' language. This does not mean, however, that there is no role for the L1 in students' personal or academic development, especially during language-focused learning activities (Goldenberg, 2008).

If teachers can understand the students' L1, they may be able to draw attention to ways in which L1 and L2 are similar or different, thus promoting L2 learning. If students occasionally use the L1 as they try to work out something new, the teacher can respond by helping them find the L2 resources they need to express their questions. When teachers do not know the students' L1, they may still be able to help them reflect on how something is said in the two languages so that they can build on the knowledge they already have of how language works.

10 In CBLT, students should be discouraged from using their L1.

Students' L1 is a central part of their identity (Cummins & Early, 2011). They should be encouraged to continue using their L1 at home and in the cultural activities of their community. Students' L1 should always be treated with respect, both inside and outside the classroom. No one should ever be made to feel ashamed or fearful when using the language they learned from their parents (Cook, 2001; Wong Fillmore, 2000).

In the L2 classroom, students' L1 is a source of knowledge about language. In some cases, students have also built up their academic knowledge through L1 education. Such knowledge should be seen as something L2 learners can build on as they acquire the new language and continue learning academic content.

CBLT teachers often express concern that when students interact with other students who have the same L1, they will not make the effort to use the L2 to complete tasks or activities but will instead 'fall back' on their L1, thereby limiting their L2 learning. The research we have read suggests two ways to respond to this concern. First, group- and pair-work tasks need to be structured in such a way that successful completion of the activity requires students to learn and use appropriate L2 vocabulary and language patterns. On the way to the completion of the activity, however, the L1 may be used to enhance and to check understanding, as we saw in the use of Spanish among students in Spotlight Study 3.1 and Classroom Snapshot 3.4. Second, group- and pair-work activities need to be appropriate to students' ability. If the task is too difficult, they may become frustrated and essentially 'drop out' of the task, using the L1 in non-productive ways. This is discussed further under statement 11 below.

11 Cooperative learning and other types of group-work are not appropriate for CBLT, especially if students have the same L1.

We have seen a number of examples from classrooms where students have worked together successfully, increasing opportunities for both language and content learning. In some of the examples, students with the same L1 were able to use that shared knowledge to work out problems and confirm their understanding of the academic content. Nevertheless, it is essential to make sure that group-work tasks and activities are designed so that students have the resources to find correct answers to their questions and that the level of language required for the task is within their reach. Without these features, a cooperative activity can become frustrating and counterproductive (Gibbons, 2002).

12 It is important to explicitly teach students the special language features that are typical of different academic subject matter.

As a rule, CBLT students need to learn the language styles and registers that are typical of both social interaction and academic discourse. Some language features are the same in both contexts, but others are different, and students need to know when it is appropriate to use one way of speaking and when to use another (Scarcella, 2011).

The vocabulary and the sentence patterns that are associated with academic discourse include some that are common to a variety of disciplines. Others are closely associated with only one discipline and must be learned within the context of reading and talking about that discipline. A number of researchers, including many who apply insights from systemic functional linguistics, have found ways to help teachers and students discover both the specialized vocabularies and specialized sentence patterns of a discipline and also to understand how those patterns reflect the meanings that are essential in understanding academic content in that discipline (Schleppegrell, 2004).

13 CBLT works when students' L1 is a language that is similar to the language of instruction (for example, English and French) rather than when the languages are very different (for example, Chinese and English).

Research on language acquisition certainly confirms that it is somewhat easier to learn a language that is very similar to one we already know. The existence of cognate vocabulary as well as similar word-order patterns and grammatical markers can give learners a head start in learning the new one.

However, good CBLT teaching has given learners the opportunity to acquire high levels of skill in the L2, even when L1 and L2 are quite dissimilar. Learners may need more time and more explicit guidance in discovering the patterns and learning the vocabulary of a language that is very different from the one they know, and CBLT can be an effective tool in this process.

14 Only native speakers of the language of instruction can be successful CBLT teachers.

Successful CBLT programs exist in a variety of environments, including some where no native speakers are available to teach. It is often the case that the teachers with the best knowledge of the subject matter are not those with the best proficiency in the language that is to be used for instruction. Nevertheless, with adequate professional development opportunities, many teachers can learn strategies that allow them to provide the kinds of activities that further students' learning of both language and content (Kong & Hoare, 2011). Teachers' own experience as language learners can give them insight into the challenges students are facing and help them understand what students are trying to say and help them say it better.

In some cases, CBLT is implemented by a team of teachers. Both teachers use the students' L2 for teaching, but the content teacher's lessons emphasize meaning-focused content learning while a teacher who has been trained for language teaching can emphasize language-focused activities. This arrangement will be most effective if the teachers coordinate their instruction to ensure that what is learned in the language-focused lessons may be practiced in the content-focused ones.

Conclusion

Learning a second language and cognitively challenging age-appropriate academic content at the same time is difficult. Teaching cognitively challenging academic content in a second language is equally so. The notion that students in classrooms where the L2 is used to teach subject matter can reach native-like levels of L2 mastery in a matter of months is based on a lack of understanding of what it takes to acquire a second language and what it means to develop a deep understanding of academic information and ways of thinking about that information. It is clear from the research on CBLT in classrooms around the world that students and teachers have to work harder than their peers to accomplish the dual goal.

It's worth the effort. For minority-language children and adolescents, effective CBLT makes the difference between academic success and failure. For majority-language students, effective CBLT leads to a level of bilingualism that is rarely achieved by students in regular foreign language programs. Students and teachers who work together to make their programs successful should feel a justifiable pride in their accomplishment.

Suggestions for Further Reading

There is a wealth of literature on CBLT, some of it focused on pedagogical practice and some on research. Choosing a limited number of items to recommend is not easy, but the ones listed below provide a good foundation in both the history and development of this approach to educating second language learners.

Echevarria, J., Vogt, M., & Short, D. J. (2012). *Making content comprehensible for English language learners: The SIOP model, fourth edition.* Boston: Pearson/Allyn and Bacon.

Based on research and professional development experience in the sheltered instruction model, the authors provide guidance for making challenging academic content accessible to L2 learners. This book is the first in a series written by these authors and introduces the SIOP (Sheltered Instruction Observation Protocol) model as it applies to teaching English language learners in US schools. Others in the series focus on particular grade levels or on particular content areas. The books will be especially useful for mainstream teachers in US schools, but the principles and many of the specific pedagogical suggestions are relevant to CBLT teachers in other contexts as well.

Genesee, F. (Ed.). (1987). *Learning through two languages.* Cambridge, MA: Newbury House.

For those interested in the history of immersion education, this book is essential reading. Genesee traces the history of Canadian immersion and provides a comprehensive review of the different program types and the findings of two decades of assessment and evaluation of them. In addition, he contrasts the social context and educational challenges in Canadian programs with those present in programs for educating minority-language children in the USA.

Genesee, F. (Ed.). (1999). Program alternatives for linguistically diverse students. Educational Practice Report No. 1. Santa Cruz, CA & Washington, DC: Center for Research on Education, Diversity and Excellence.

This report provides a clear overview of the options for minority-language students in the USA in the 1990s. Even though changes to education law have altered the availability of some of the programs, the descriptions of them remain valuable, if only for understanding what is lost when some of these options are restricted. Each program type is described, using the same template to cover aspects such the pedagogical approach, the program goals, and the local conditions that establish the context for implementation.

Gibbons, P. (2002). *Scaffolding language, scaffolding learning: Teaching second language learners in the mainstream classroom*. Portsmouth, NH: Heinemann.

Essential reading for teachers who work with young L2 learners in CBLT classrooms. Rich with examples of teacher–learner and learner–learner interaction as well as suggestions for classroom tasks and activities, the text reflects the author's extensive experience as a teacher and teacher educator. Grounded in research and theory, but thoroughly practical, it will be of value not only to those teaching in the mainstream (as the title suggests) but for any teacher who has responsibility for helping learners acquire both a second language and academic content. Many of the ideas in this book are elaborated further in Gibbons (2009).

Goldenberg, C. (2008). Teaching English language learners: What the research does—and does not—say. *American Educator, Summer*. 8–23, 42–4.

In this concise, readable, and informative overview of research on the education of English language learners in the USA, Goldenberg has summarized the report of the National Literacy Panel (August & Shanahan, 2008) in a way that makes the main findings—and the remaining questions—understandable and compelling. The article also includes numerous links to websites that expand on pedagogical implications of the research. The article is also rich in specific examples of classroom learning and teaching.

Graves, M. F., August, D., & Mancilla-Martínez, J. (2013) *Teaching vocabulary to English language learners*. New York: Teachers College Press.

This volume combines information drawn from the large body of research on the education of English Language Learners in the US.

In addition, the writers propose a four-part approach to vocabulary teaching that is designed to help second language learners from beginning to advanced stages.

A valuable translation of research findings for classroom practice.

Lyster, R. (2007). *Learning and teaching language through content: A counterbalanced approach*. Amsterdam: John Benjamins.

This review of research on content-based language teaching focuses on the effects on learning of the pedagogical practices that have been observed in many classrooms. Lyster shows how pedagogical practices that are effective in some contexts may be less effective in others and argues for a 'counterbalanced approach' to instruction and feedback through which teachers can guide learners to focus on both language and content.

Richard-Amato, P. A. & **Snow, M. A.** (Eds.). (1992). *The multicultural classroom: Readings for content-area teachers*. Reading, MA: Addison Wesley.

The 26 chapters in this collection were written by teachers and researchers whose insights into CBLT are practical and grounded in both experience and reflection. The chapters are divided into four main parts: 1) theoretical foundations, 2) cultural considerations, 3) instructional practices and materials for the classroom, and 4) applications of CBLT in specific content areas. Each chapter is accompanied by follow-up questions and activities that allow readers to reflect further on a topic. Some of the chapters in this 1992 book were first published in the 1980s. Yet this remains one of the most informative and inspirational resources for teachers who are new to CBLT and an important reminder of the excellent work that teachers and researchers have done in this area for a long time.

Tedick, D. J., Christian, D., & **Fortune, T. W.** (Eds.). (2011). *Immersion education: Practices, policies, possibilities*. Bristol, UK: Multilingual Matters.

Tedick and her colleagues bring together researchers and educators to report on aspects of immersion education in schools around the world—from Finland to China, Hawai'i to Ireland. This book builds on the earlier work published in Fortune and Tedick's (2008) book, *Pathways to multilingualism: Evolving perspectives on immersion education*. Both books show how immersion programs share opportunities and challenges

Glossary

academic content: the information and ways of thinking that students are expected to acquire and retain about subject matter such as history, science, mathematics, and literature.

academic language: the vocabulary, sentence patterns, text organization, and style of speaking and writing that are used in educational or professional environments.

academic vocabulary: words that occur in texts about academic and technical subject matter. Some words are specific to a particular field; others spear in the texts of many different disciplines.

academic word list: in English, a list of 570 words that occur in texts in a number of different disciplines but are not specific to any one discipline (see Coxhead, 2000).

additive bilingualism: learning a second language without losing the first.

automatic: spontaneous, unstoppable, not requiring time for reflection.

BICS (Basic Interpersonal Communication Skills): the ability to use language for informal, conversational interactions.

bilingual education: any approach to schooling in which more than one language is used in teaching and learning academic content.

CALP (Cognitive Academic Language Proficiency): the ability to use language to learn about academic content through listening and reading and to communicate about this content through speaking and writing, using technical vocabulary and language patterns at an age-appropriate level.

CBLT (Content-Based Language Teaching): instruction provided to students who are learning both the academic content and the language in which the content is taught.

CLIL (Content and Language Integrated Learning): a CBLT approach that has been developed to expand L2 learning opportunities, especially for students in European secondary schools.

comprehensible input hypothesis: Krashen's hypothesis that L2 acquisition occurs when L2 listeners/readers are exposed to language they can understand and which contains a small amount of new language.

comprehensible output hypothesis: Swain's hypothesis that L2 acquisition is furthered when speakers/writers attempt to express themselves. When they discover that they do not have the linguistic resources to do so, they look for new language to fill the gap.

content: see academic content.

content-obligatory language: the vocabulary, phrases, sentence patterns, and styles that are required in a particular academic subject.

content-compatible language: the vocabulary, phrases, sentence patterns, and styles that are typical in a particular academic subject.

cooperative learning: working in pairs or groups on a task that requires each participant to contribute specific information or procedures.

core French: French as second language instruction that is designed to teach the language in periods of a few hours each week. Contrasts with extended French and French immersion approaches.

corrective feedback: information that tells speakers or writers whether what they have said or written has been understood and whether it is accurate and appropriate.

developmental sequence: the order in which particular knowledge or skill is acquired.

direct instruction: explicit teaching on a particular content or process, including language.

dual immersion: an approach to CBLT that places proficient speakers and learners of two different languages in combined classrooms and provides content instruction in both languages to both groups. Also called 'two-way immersion'.

ELL (English language learner): the term often used to describe a student in a US school who has not met the age-appropriate proficiency goals of particular standardized tests.

encoding: the internalization of information. In cognitive psychology, the term is synonymous with the first stage of learning. Information must be encoded so that it can be used in working memory and eventually stored in long-term memory.

extended French: CBLT instruction in which second language learners are taught one or two academic subjects in French and continue to study French
as a subject.

first language: the language that was acquired first in a person's life. Also referred to as home language or L1. In some situations, an individual may have more than one L1. That person would be called a simultaneous bilingual.

fluency: automatic, apparently effortless use of language. Fluency is a goal for listening, reading, and writing as well as speaking.

foreign language: a language (also referred to as second language or L2) that is not ordinarily spoken among people in a learner's local environment. It is used in this book to refer to a lack of opportunities to use the language outside class rather than the legal status of a language in a particular country.

immersion: a program of content-based instruction in a foreign language for students who share the same L1.

interlanguage: patterns in the knowledge and use of a language by a person who is in the process of learning that language.

L1: see first language

L2: see second language and foreign language

language-focused instruction: instruction that draws L2 learners' attention to the language itself.

language-related episode (LRE): an interaction in which learners who are engaged in a communicative task or activity turn their attention to the language itself.

literacy: the ability to read and write but also the ability to understand and interpret language in a variety of contexts, especially those requiring knowledge of academic language.

mainstream: instruction designed for students who are already proficient speakers of the language used in the instruction.

majority language: the language that is most widely spoken in a particular region.

minority language: the language spoken by those who are less numerous. The term is also sometimes used to refer to the language spoken by those with less status or political power.

Nation's four strands: a framework for providing second- or foreign-language instruction that includes the range of activities and processing types that are deemed necessary for language acquisition to occur.

native speaker: a language user who has reached a high level of proficiency in a language, typically one who began using the language from an early age.

peer interaction: in a classroom, conversation or tasks that involve students working with each other.

proficiency: the level of ability an individual has in using a language. Often discussed in terms of performance on standardized tests.

pull-out: an approach to L2 instruction in which learners are taken out of their content-based lessons for specific instruction in the language itself for a certain period in each day or week.

push-in: an approach to supporting L2 learners in which an additional teacher works with them in their regular content-based classroom.

qualitative research: research that aims to describe and understand an environment and the processes that occur in it.

quantitative research: research based on explicitly measuring variables and, often, using statistical analysis to identify relationships among them.

recast: feedback that repeats a learner's utterance, keeping the meaning but correcting any errors.

retrieval: the process of recalling something that has been learned.

scaffolding: supporting the communicative efforts of another speaker, especially a language learner, by providing vocabulary or partial sentences that the speaker can 'build' on.

second language (L2): a language learned after the first language (L1) has been acquired. In some contexts, a distinction will be made between the terms second language (a language that is used in everyday communication outside the classroom) and foreign language (a language used only or primarily in the classroom).

sheltered content instruction: teaching that is adapted to the needs of L2 learners, employing pedagogical strategies and materials that allow L2 learners to access academic content appropriate for their age level.

skill learning: an approach to learning described by cognitive psychologists: learning begins with attention to what needs to be learned and, through practice, the learner acquires the ability to use the skill automatically.

specific language impairment: an inability to acquire language at the typical rate and in the typical way by children whose cognitive and physical development are otherwise typical.

structured English immersion: an approach to teaching language to L2 learners that is based on the hypothesis that an intensive course in the language is needed to prepare students for content-based instruction.

submersion: placement of L2 learners in classrooms where all or most other students already have age-appropriate proficiency in the language of instruction.

target forms: forms of the language being learned.

transfer-appropriate processing: learning that occurs in an environment that is similar to the one where what is learned will later be used.

working memory: the mental processes that an individual uses in focusing on information or activities at a given time. Contrasts with long-term memory, which is thought of as a metaphorical place to store what has been learned.

References

Arkoudis, S. (2006). Negotiating the rough ground between ESL and mainstream teachers. *International Journal of Bilingual Education and Bilingualism, 9*, 415–33.

Allen, P., Fröhlich, M., & Spada, N. (1984). The communicative orientation of language teaching: an observation scheme. In J. Handscombe, R. A. Orem, & B. P. Taylor (Eds.). *On TESOL '83*. Washington, DC: TESOL.

Antón, M., & Di Camilla, F. (1998). Socio–cognitive functions of L1 collaborative interaction in the L2 classroom. *Canadian Modern Language Review, 54*, 314–42.

August, D., & Shanahan, T. (Eds.). (2008). *Developing reading and writing in second-language learners: Lessons from the report of the National Literacy Panel on Language-Minority Children and Youth*. New York: Routledge.

Baetens Beardsmore, H. (Ed.). (1993). *European models of bilingual education*. Clevedon, UK: Multilingual Matters.

Ballinger, S., & Lyster, R. (2011). Student and teacher oral language use in a two-way Spanish/English immersion school. *Language Teaching Research, 15*, 289–306.

Bardovi-Harlig, K. (2009). Conventional expressions as a pragmalinguistics resource: Recognition and production of conventional expressions in L2 pragmatics. *Language Learning 59*, 755–95.

Beck, I. L., McKeown, M. G., & Kucan, L. (2002). *Bringing words to life: Robust vocabulary instruction*. New York: The Guilford Press.

Benjamin, A., & Crow, J. T. (2010). *Vocabulary at the center*. Larchmont, NY: Eye on Education.

Benson, C. (2004). Bilingual education in Mozambique and Bolivia: From experimentation to implementation. *Language Policy, 3*, 47–66.

Bialystok E. (2007). Cognitive effects of bilingualism: How linguistic experience leads to cognitive change. *International Journal of Bilingual Education and Bilingualism, 10*, 210–23.

Bibeau, G. (1982). *L'éducation bilingue en Amérique du Nord*. Montreal: Guérin.

Bjork, R. (1994). Memory and metamemory considerations in the training of human beings. In J. Metcalfe & A. Shimamura (Eds.). *Metacognition: Knowing about knowing* (pp. 185–205). Cambridge, MA: MIT Press.

Bransford, J. D., & Johnson, M. K. (1972). Contextual prerequisites for understanding: Some investigations of comprehension and recall. *Journal of Verbal Learning and Verbal Behavior, 11*, 717–26.

Brinton, D., Sasser, L., & Winningham, B. (1992). Language minority students in multicultural classrooms. In P. A. Richard-Amato & M. A. Snow (Eds.), *The multicultural classroom: Readings for content-area teachers* (pp. 5–15). Reading, MA: Addison-Wesley.

Bruton, A. (2011). Is CLIL so beneficial, or just selective? Reevaluating some of the research. *System, 39,* 523–32.

Calderón, M. E., & Minaya-Rowe, L. (2003). *Designing and implementing two-way bilingual programs: A step-by-step guide for administrators, teachers, and parents.* Thousand Oaks, CA: Corwin Press.

Calvé, P. (1986). L'immersion au secondaire: bilan et perspectives. *CONTACT, 5,* 21–8.

Chall, J. S., & Jacobs, V. A. (2003). The classic study on poor children's fourth-grade slump. *American Educator*, Spring, 2003. http://www.aft.org/pubsreports/american_educator/spring2003/chall.html. Retrieved May 11, 2012.

Chamot, A. U., Cummins, J., Kessler, C., O'Malley, J. M., Wong Fillmore, L. (1997). *Accelerating English Language Learning, Book 3.* Glenview, IL: Scott Foresman.

Chimbutane, F. (2011). *Rethinking bilingual education in postcolonial contexts.* Bristol, UK: Multilingual Matters.

Christian, D., Montone, C., Lindholm, K., & Carranza, I. (1997). *Profiles in two-way immersion education.* McHenry, IL: Delta Systems and Center for Applied Linguistics.

Clark, K. (2009). The case for structured immersion. *Educational Leadership, 66,* 42–6. pdf retrieved May 4, 2012.

Cohen, A., & Swain, M. (1976). Bilingual education: The 'immersion' model in the North American context. *TESOL Quarterly, 10,* 45–53.

Collier, V. P. (1987). Age and rate of acquisition of second language for academic purposes. *TESOL Quarterly, 21*, 617–741.

Collier, V. P. (1989). How long? A synthesis of research on academic achievement in second language. *TESOL Quarterly, 23*, 509–31.

Collier, V. P. (Fall, 1995). Acquiring a second language for school. *Directions in Language & Education, 1,* no. 4. National Clearinghouse for Bilingual Education.

Collier, V. P. , & Thomas, W. P. (2004). The astounding effectiveness of dual language education for all. *NABE Journal of Research and Practice*, 2, 1–20.

Collins, L., & White, J. (2011). An intensive look at intensity and language learning. *TESOL Quarterly*, *45,* 106–33.

Collins, L., Halter, R., Lightbown, P. M., & Spada, N. (1999). Time and the distribution of time in second language instruction. *TESOL Quarterly, 33,* 655–80.

Cook, V. (2001). Using the first language in the classroom. *Canadian Modern Language Review, 57,* 402–23.

Cook, V. (2008). *Second language learning and language teaching, fourth edition.* London: Hodder Education.

Coxhead, A. (2000). A new academic word list. *TESOL Quarterly, 34(2)*: 213–18.

Coyle, D., & Baetens Beardsmore, H. (Eds.). (2007). Research on content and language integrated learning (CLIL). *International Journal of Bilingual Education and Bilingualism: Special issue, 10* (5).

Coyle, D., Hood, P., & Marsh, D. (2010). *CLIL: Content and language integrated learning*. Cambridge: Cambridge University Press.

Crago, M. (1992). Communicative interaction and second language acquisition: An Inuit example. *TESOL Quarterly, 26*, 487–505.

Craik, F. I. M. (2002). Levels of processing: Past, present … and future? *Memory, 10*, 305–18.

Crandall, J. (Ed.). (1987). *ESL through content-area instruction*. Englewood Cliffs, NJ: Prentice-Hall Regents.

Crawford, J. (2008). *Advocating for English learners: Selected essays*. Clevedon, UK: Multilingual Matters.

Creese, A. (2005). *Teacher collaboration and talk in multilingual classrooms*. Clevedon, UK: Multilingual Matters.

Cummins, J. (1980). The entry and exit fallacy in bilingual education. *NABE Journal, 4*, 25–60.

Cummins, J. (1984). *Bilingualism and special education: Issues in assessment and pedagogy*. Clevedon, UK: Multilingual Matters.

Cummins, J. (2000). *Language, power, and pedagogy: Bilingual children in the crossfire*. Clevedon, UK: Multilingual Matters.

Cummins, J. (2002). Reading and the ESL student. *Orbit, 33*, 19–22.

Cummins, J., & Early, M. (Eds.). (2011). *Identity texts: The collaborative creation of power in multilingual schools*. Oakhill, UK: Trentham Books.

Dalton-Puffer, C. (2007). *Discourse in content-and-language-integrated learning (CLIL) classrooms*. New York, Amsterdam: Benjamins.

Dalton-Puffer, C. (2011). Content and language integrated learning: From practice to principles? *Annual Review of Applied Linguistics, 31*, 182–204.

Davison, C. (2006). Collaboration between ESL and content teachers: How do we know when we are doing it right? *The International Journal of Bilingual Education and Bilingualism, 9*, 454–75.

de Courcy, M. C. (2002). *Learners' experiences of immersion education: Case studies in French and Chinese*. Clevedon, UK: Multilingual Matters.

DeGraaff, R., Koopman, G. J., & G. Westhoff. (2007). Identifying effective L2 pedagogy in content and language integrated learning (CLIL). Vienna English Working Papers 16, no. 3: 12–19.

de Jong, E. & Howard, E. (2009). Integration in two-way immersion education: Equalising linguistic benefits for all students. *International Journal of Bilingual Education and Bilingualism, 12*, 81–99.

DeKeyser, R. (1998). Beyond focus on form: Cognitive perspectives on learning and practicing second language grammar. In C. Doughty & J. Williams (Eds.), *Focus on form in classroom second language acquisition* (pp. 42–63). Cambridge: Cambridge University Press.

DeKeyser, R. (2007). Introduction: Situating the concept of practice. In R. DeKeyser (Ed.), *Practice in a second language: Perspectives from applied linguistics and cognitive psychology* (pp. 1–20). Cambridge: Cambridge University Press.

Dempster, F. N. (1996). Distributing and managing the conditions of encoding and practice. In E. Bjork, & R. A. Bjork (Eds.), *Memory Volume 10: Handbook of perception and cognition* (pp. 317–44). New York: Academic Press.

DePalma, R. (2010). *Language use in the two-way classroom: Lessons from a Spanish–English bilingual kindergarten.* Bristol, UK: Multilingual Matters.

Dixon, L. Q., Zhao, J., Shin, J.-Y., Wu, S., Su, J.-H., Burgess-Brigham, R., Gezer, M. U., & Snow, C. (2012). What we know about second language acquisition: A synthesis from four perspectives. *Review of Educational Research, 82,* 5–60.

Donato, R. (2004). Aspects of collaboration in pedagogical discourse. *Annual Review of Applied Linguistics, 24,* 284–302.

Doughty, C., & Varela, E. (1998). Communicative focus on form. In C. Doughty & J. Williams (Eds.), *Focus on form in second language classrooms* (pp. 114–38). New York: Cambridge University Press.

Echevarria, J., & Graves, A. (2007). *Sheltered content instruction: Teaching English-language learners with diverse abilities, third edition.* Boston: Allyn and Bacon.

Echevarria, J., Vogt, M., & Short, D. J. (2012). *Making content comprehensible for English language learners: The SIOP model, fourth edition.* Boston: Pearson/Allyn and Bacon.

Ellis, N. (2002). Frequency effects in language processing: A review with implications for theories of implicit and explicit language acquisition. *Studies in Second Language Acquisition, 24,* 143–88.

Ellis, N. (2009). Optimizing the input: Frequency and sampling in usage-based and form-focused learning. In C. J. Doughty and M. H. Long (Eds.), *The handbook of language teaching* (pp. 139–58). Malden, MA: Wiley-Blackwell.

Fazio, L., & Lyster, R. (1998). Immersion and submersion classrooms: A comparison of instructional practices in language arts. *Journal of Multilingual and Multicultural Development, 19,* 303–17.

Fortune, T. W. (2004). Scaffolding techniques in CBI classrooms. (Online at the CoBaLTT website)

Fortune, T. W., with Menke, M. R. (2010). *Struggling learners and language immersion education: Research-based, practitioner-informed responses to educators' top questions* (CARLA Publication Series). Minneapolis, MN: The University of Minnesota, The Center for Advanced Research on Language Acquisition.

Fortune, T. W., & Tedick, D. J. (Eds.). (2008). *Pathways to multilingualism: Evolving perspectives on immersion education.* Clevedon, UK: Multilingual Matters.

Fortune, T. W., Tedick, D. J., & Walker, C. L. (2008). Integrated language and content teaching: Insights from the language immersion classroom. In Fortune, T., & Tedick, D. J. (Eds.), *Pathways to multilingualism: Evolving perspectives on immersion education.* (pp. 71–96). Clevedon, UK: Multilingual Matters.

Fu, D. (2009). *Writing between languages: How English language learners make the transition to fluency. Grades 4–12*. Portsmouth, NH: Heinemann.
Gardner, D. (2004). Vocabulary input through extensive reading: A comparison of words found in children's narrative and expository reading materials. *Applied Linguistics, 25*, 1–37.
Gardner, D. (2008). Vocabulary recycling in children's authentic reading materials: A corpus-based investigation of narrow reading. *Reading in a Foreign Language, 20*, 92–122.
Gatbonton, E., & **Segalowitz, N.** (2005). Rethinking communicative language teaching: A focus on ACCESS to fluency. *Canadian Modern Language Review, 61*, 325–53.
Genesee, F. (1987). *Learning through two languages: Studies of immersion and bilingual education*. New York: Newbury House.
Genesee, F. (Ed.). (1999). Program alternatives for linguistically diverse students. Educational Practice Report No. 1. Santa Cruz, CA & Washington, DC: CREDE: Center for Research on Education, Diversity and Excellence. pdf available at http://www.cal.org/crede/pubs/edpracreports.html#8
Genesee, F. (2004). What do we know about bilingual education for majority language students? In T. K. Bhatia and W. Ritchie (Eds.), *Handbook of Bilingualism and Multiculturalism* (pp. 547–76). Malden, MA: Blackwell.
Genesee, F., **Geva, E.**, **Dressler, C.**, & **Kamil, M. L.** (2008). Cross-linguistic relationships in second-language learners. In D. August & T. Shanahan (Eds.), *Developing reading and writing in second-language learners: Lessons from the report of the National Literacy Panel on Language–Minority Children and Youth*. New York: Routledge.
Gibbons, P. (2002). *Scaffolding language, scaffolding learning*. Portsmouth, NH: Heinemann.
Gibbons, P. (2009). *English learners, academic literacy, and thinking: Learning in the challenge zone*. Portsmouth, NH: Heinemann.
Goldenberg, C. (2008). Teaching English language learners: What the research does—and does not—say. *American Educator*, Summer. 8–23, 42–4. www.edweek.org/media/ell_final.pdf
Goldschneider, J., & **DeKeyser, R.** (2001). Explaining the 'Natural Order of L2 morpheme acquisition' in English: A meta-analysis of multiple determinants. *Language Learning, 51*, 1–50.
Gooch, L. (2009, July 8). Malaysia ends use of English in science and math teaching. *New York Times*.
Graves, M. F., **August, D.**, & **Mancilla-Martínez, J.** (2013) *Teaching vocabulary to English language learners*. New York: Teachers College Press.
Hakuta, K. (1986). *Mirror of language: The debate on bilingualism*. New York: Basic Books, Inc.
Halliday, M. A. K. (2004). *An introduction to functional grammar, third edition* (revised by C. Matthiessen). London: Arnold.

Hamayan, E. (1994). Language development of low-literacy students. In F. Genesee (Ed.), *Educating second language children: The whole child, the whole curriculum, the whole community* (pp. 278–300). Cambridge: Cambridge University Press.

Harley, B. (1998). The role of focus-on-form tasks in promoting child L2 acquisition. In C. Doughty & J. Williams (Eds.), *Focus on form in classroom second language acquisition* (pp. 156–73). Cambridge: Cambridge University Press.

Harley, B., & Swain, M. (1984). The interlanguage of immersion students and its implications for second language teaching. In A. Davies, C. Criper, & A. P. R. Howatt (Eds.), *Interlanguage* (pp. 291–311). Edinburgh: Edinburgh University Press.

Hawkins, E. (1988). *Intensive language teaching and learning: Initiatives at the school level.* London: Centre for Information on Language Teaching Research.

Hickey, T. (2001). Mixing beginners and native speakers in minority language immersion: Who is immersing whom? *Canadian Modern Language Review, 57*, 443–74.

Hinkel, E. (2012, February). Language teaching and construction grammar. *AL Forum: The Newsletter of the (TESOL) Applied Linguistics Interest Section.*

Hoare, P. (2010). Content-based language teaching in China: Contextual influences on implementation. *Journal of Multilingual and Multicultural Development, 31*, 69–86.

Hoare, P., & Kong, S. (2008). Late immersion in Hong Kong: Still stressed but making progress? In T. W. Fortune & D. J. Tedick (Eds.), *Pathways to multilingualism: Emerging perspectives on immersion education* (pp. 242–63). Clevedon, UK: Multilingual Matters.

Hornberger, N. (2002). Multilingual language policies and the continua of biliteracy: An ecological approach. *Language Policy, 1*, 27–51. Reprinted in O. García & C. Baker (Eds.) (2007), *Bilingual education: An introductory reader* (pp. 177–94). Clevedon, UK: Multilingual Matters.

Horst, M. (2005). Vocabulary learning through extensive reading. *Canadian Modern Language Review, 61*, 355–82.

Housen, A. (2002a). Second language achievement in the European School system of multilingual education. In D. So & G. Jones (Eds.), *Education and society in plurilingual contexts* (pp. 96–128). Brussels/London: VUB Press/Longman.

Housen, A. (2002b). Processes and outcomes in the European Schools model of multilingual education. *Bilingual Research Journal, 26*, 43–62.

Housen, A. (2012). Time and amount of L2 contact inside and outside the school—Insights from the European Schools. In C. Muñoz (Ed.), *Intensive exposure experiences in SL learning* (pp. 111–38). Bristol, UK: Multilingual Matters.

Housen, A., Schoonjans, E., Janssens, S., Welcomme, A. Schoonheere, E., & Pierrard, M. (2011). Conceptualizing and measuring the impact of contextual factors in instructed SLA—the role of language prominence. *International Review of Applied Linguistics, 49*, 83–112.

Howard, E. R., Sugarman, J., & Christian, D. (2003). *Trends in two-way immersion education: A review of the research.* Washington, DC: Center for Applied Linguistics.

Hulstijn, J., Hollander, M., & Greidanus, T. (1996). Incidental vocabulary learning by advanced foreign language students: The influence of marginal glosses, dictionary use, and reoccurrence of unknown words. *The Modern Language Journal, 80*, 327–39.

Johnson, R. K., & Swain, M. (Eds.). (1997). *Immersion education: International perspectives.* Cambridge: Cambridge University Press.

Kaufman, D., & Crandall, J. A. (Eds.). (2005). *Content-based instruction in elementary and secondary school settings.* Alexandria, VA: TESOL.

Kaufman, D. & Crandall, J. A. (Eds.). (2005). *Case studies in content-based instruction for elementary and secondary school settings.* Alexandria, VA: TESOL.

Kinsella, K. (1997). Moving from comprehensible input to "learning to learn" in content-based instruction. In M. A. Snow & D. M. Brinton (Eds.), *The content-based classroom: Perspectives on integrating language and content* (pp. 46–68). White Plains, NY: Longman.

Klingner, J. R., & Vaughn, S. (2000). The helping behaviors of fifth graders while using collaborative strategic reading during ESL content classes. *TESOL Quarterly, 34*, 69–98.

Kohnert, K. (2007). *Language disorders in bilingual children and adults.* San Diego, CA: Plural.

Kong, S. (2008). Late immersion in Hong Kong: A pedagogical framework for integrating content–language teaching and learning. *The Journal of Asia TEFL, 5*, 107–32.

Kong, S. (2009). Content-based instruction: What can we learn from content-trained teachers' and language-trained teachers' pedagogies? *Canadian Modern Language Review,* 66, 233–67.

Kong, S., & Hoare, P. (2011). Cognitive content engagement in content-based language teaching. *Language Teaching Research, 15*, 307–24.

Kowal, M., & Swain, M. (1997). From semantic to syntactic processing: How can we promote it in the immersion classroom? In R. K. Johnson & M. Swain (Eds.), *Immersion education: International perspectives* (pp. 284–309). Cambridge: Cambridge University Press.

Krashen, S. (1989). We acquire vocabulary and spelling from reading: Additional evidence for the input hypothesis. *The Modern Language Journal, 73*, 440–64.

Krashen, S., Rolstad, K., & MacSwan, J. (2007). *Review of 'Research Summary and Bibliography for Structured English Immersion Programs' of the Arizona English Language Learners Task Force.* pdf retrieved May 4, 2012.

Lambert, W. E., & Tucker, G. R. (1972). *Bilingual education of children: The St. Lambert experiment.* Rowley, MA: Newbury House.

Lasagabaster, D. (2008). Foreign language competence in content and language integrated courses. *The Open Applied Linguistics Journal, 1*, 30–41.

Lessow-Hurley, J. (2013). *The foundations of dual language instruction, sixth edition.* New York: Pearson.

Lightbown, P. M. (1990). Process–product research on second language learning in classrooms. In B. Harley, P. Allen, J. Cummins, & M. Swain (Eds.), *The development of second language proficiency* (pp. 82–92). Cambridge: Cambridge University Press.

Lightbown, P. M. (1998). The importance of timing in focus on form. In C. Doughty and J. Williams (Eds.), *Focus on form in classroom second language acquisition* (pp. 177–96). Cambridge: Cambridge University Press.

Lightbown, P. M. (2007). Fair trade: Two-way bilingual education. *Estudios de Lingüística Inglesa Aplicada, 7:* 9–34.

Lightbown, P. M. (2008a). Easy as pie? Children learning languages. *Concordia Working Papers in Applied Linguistics, 1*, 1–25. http://doe.concordia.ca/copal/index.php/copal/volumes.html

Lightbown, P. M. (2008b). Transfer-appropriate processing as a model for classroom second language acquisition. In Z. Han (Ed.), *Understanding second language process* (pp. 27–44). Clevedon, UK: Multilingual Matters.

Lightbown, P. M. (2012). Intensive L2 instruction in Canada: Why not immersion? In C. Muñoz (Ed.), *Intensive exposure experiences in SL learning* (pp. 25–44). Bristol, UK: Multilingual Matters.

Lightbown, P. M., & Spada, N. (1991). Étude à long terme de l'apprentissage intensif de l'anglais, langue seconde, au primaire. *Canadian Modern Language Review, 53*, 315–55.

Lightbown, P. M., & Spada, N. (1994). An innovative program for primary ESL in Quebec. *TESOL Quarterly, 28*, 563–79.

Lightbown, P. M., & Spada, N. (2013). *How languages are learned, fourth edition.* Oxford: Oxford University Press.

Lindholm-Leary, K. (2001). *Dual language education.* Clevedon, UK: Multilingual Matters.

Lindholm-Leary, K. (2011). Student outcomes in Chinese two-way immersion programs: Language proficiency, academic achievement and student attitudes. In D. J. Tedick, D. Christian, and T. W. Fortune (Eds.), *Immersion education: Practices, policies, possibilities* (pp. 81–103). Bristol, UK: Multilingual Matters.

Lindholm-Leary, K., & Block, N. (2010). Achievement in predominantly low SES/Hispanic schools. *International Journal of Bilingualism and Bilingual Education, 13*, 43–60.

Lindholm-Leary, K., & Borsato, G. (2006). Academic achievement. In F. Genesee, K. Lindholm-Leary, W. M. Saunders, & D. Christian (Eds.), *Educating English language learners: A synthesis of research evidence* (pp. 176–222). New York: Cambridge.

Loewen, S., Li, S., Fei, F., Thompson, A., Nakatsukasa, K., Ahn, S., and Chen, X. (2009). Second language learners' beliefs about grammar instruction and error correction. *Modern Language Journal, 93*, 91–104.

Long, M. (1996). The role of the linguistic environment in second language acquisition. In W. Ritchie and T. Bhatia (Eds.), *Handbook of Second Language Acquisition* (pp. 413–68). New York: Academic Press.

Lortie, D. C. (1975). *Schoolteacher: A sociological study.* Second edition published in 2002. Chicago: University of Chicago Press.

Lyster, R. (1987). Speaking immersion. *The Canadian Modern Language Review, 43*, 701–17.

Lyster, R. (1994). The effect of functional–analytic teaching on aspects of French immersion students' sociolinguistic competence. *Applied Linguistics, 15*, 263–87.

Lyster, R. (1998). Recasts, repetition, and ambiguity in L2 classroom discourse. *Studies in Second Language Acquisition, 20*, 51–81.

Lyster, R. (2001). Negotiation of form, recasts, and explicit correction in relation to error types and learner repair in immersion classrooms. *Language Learning, 51 (Supplement 1)*, 265–301.

Lyster, R. (2004). Differential effects of prompts and recasts in form-focused instruction. *Studies in Second Language Acquisition, 26*, 399–432.

Lyster, R. (2007). *Learning and teaching languages through content: A counterbalanced approach* (pp. 26–7). Amsterdam: John Benjamins.

Lyster, R. (2011). Content-based second language teaching. In E. Hinkel (Ed.), *Handbook of research in second language teaching and learning, Vol. 2.* (pp. 611–30). New York: Routledge.

Lyster, R., & Mori, H. (2006). Interactional feedback and instructional counterbalance. *Studies in Second Language Acquisition, 28*, 269–300.

Lyster, R., & Ranta, L. (1997). Corrective feedback and learner uptake: Negotiation of form in communicative classrooms. *Studies in Second Language Acquisition, 19*, 37–66.

Marsh, H. W., Hau, K.-T., & Kong, C.-K. (2000). Late immersion and language of instruction (English vs. Chinese) in Hong Kong high schools: Achievement growth in language and non-language subjects. *Harvard Educational Review, 70*, 302–46.

Marshall, P. (2011). A case study of compact core French models: A pedagogic perspective. PhD Dissertation, Ontario Institute for Studies in Education, University of Toronto.

McGroarty, M. (1989). Cooperative learning: The benefits for content-area teaching. *NABE Journal, 13*, 127–43. Reprinted in P. A. Richard-Amato & M. A. Snow (Eds.). (1992), *The multicultural classroom: Readings for content-area teachers* pp. 58–69.

Met, M. (1994). Teaching content through a second language. In F. Genesee (Ed.), *Educating second language children: The whole child, the whole curriculum, the whole community.* Cambridge: Cambridge University Press.

Met, M. (2008). Paying attention to language: Literacy, language, and academic achievement. In T. W. Fortune & D. J. Tedick (Eds.), *Pathways to multilingualism: Evolving perspectives on immersion education.* Clevedon: Multilingual Matters.

Minaya-Rowe, L. & Calderón, M. E. (2003). *Designing and implementing two-way bilingual programs.* Thousand Oaks, CA: Corwin Press, Inc.

Mohan, B. (1986). *Language and content.* Reading, MA: Addison-Wesley.

Mougeon, R., Nadasdi, T., & Rehner K. (2010). *The sociolinguistic competence of immersion students.* Bristol, UK: Multilingual Matters.

Muñoz, C. (2006). The effects of age on foreign language learning: The BAF project. In C. Muñoz (Ed.), *Age and the rate of foreign language learning.* Clevedon, UK: Multilingual Matters.

Muñoz, C. (2007a). CLIL: Some thoughts on its psycholinguistic principles. *Volume Monográfico*, 17–26.

Muñoz, C. (2007b). Age-related differences and second language learning practice. In R. DeKeyser (Ed.), *Practice in a second language: Perspectives from applied linguistics and cognitive psychology* (pp. 229–55). Cambridge: Cambridge University Press.

Nagy, W. E., Herman, P., & Anderson, R. (1985). Learning words from context. *Reading Research Quarterly, 20*, 304–30.

Nation, I. S. P. (2001). *Learning vocabulary in another language.* Cambridge: Cambridge University Press.

Nation, I. S. P. (2007). The four strands. *Innovation in Language Learning and Teaching, 1*, 2–13.

Obondo, M. A. (2007). Tensions between English and mother tongue teaching in post-colonial Africa. In J. Cummins, & C. Davison (Eds.), *International handbook of English language teaching* (pp. 37–50). New York: Springer.

Oliver, R., & Mackey, A. (2003). Interactional context and feedback in child ESL classrooms. *The Modern Language Journal, 87*, 519–33.

Oliver, R., Philp, J., & Mackey, A. (2008). The impact of teacher input, guidance and feedback on ESL children's task-based interactions. In J. Philp, R. Oliver, & A. Mackey (Eds.), *Second language acquisition and the younger learner: Child's play?* (131–47). Amsterdam: John Benjamins.

Oller, D. K., & Jarmulowicz, L. (2009). Language and literacy in bilingual children in the early school years. In E. Hoff & M. Shatz (Eds.), *Blackwell Handbook of Language Development* (pp. 368–86). Malden, MA: Wiley-Blackwell.

Pellicer-Sánchez, A., & Schmitt, N. (2010). Incidental vocabulary acquisition from an authentic novel: Do things fall apart? *Reading in a Foreign Language, 22*, 31–55.

Pérez-Cañado, M. L. (2012). CLIL research in Europe: past, present, and future. *International Journal of Bilingual Education and Bilingualism, 15*, 315–41.

Pienemann, M. (1999). *Language processing and second language development: Processability theory.* Amsterdam: John Benjamins.

Ranta, L., & Lyster, R. (2007). A cognitive approach to improving immersion students' oral language abilities: The Awareness–Practice–Feedback sequence. In R. DeKeyser (Ed.), *Practice in a second language: Perspectives from applied linguistics and cognitive psychology* (pp. 141–60). Cambridge: Cambridge University Press.

Richard-Amato, P. A., & Snow, M. A. (Eds.). (1992). *The multicultural classroom: Readings for content-area teachers*. Reading, MA: Addison-Wesley.

Ringbom, H., & Jarvis, S. (2009). The importance of cross-linguistic similarity in foreign language learning. In M. H. Long & C. J. Doughty (Eds.), *The handbook of language teaching* (pp. 106–18). Malden, MA: Wiley-Blackwell.

Roediger, H. L. & Karpicke, J. D. (2006). The power of testing memory. Basic research and implications for educational practice. *Perspectives on Psychological Science, 1*(3), 181–210.

Roever, C. (2012). What learners get for free: Learning of routine formulae in ESL and EFL environments. *ELT Journal, 66*, 10–21.

Rossel, C., & Baker, K. (1996). The educational effectiveness of bilingual education. *Research in the Teaching of English, 30*, 7–74.

Scarcella, R. (2011). *Academic Language and English Language Learners*. http://www.colorincolorado.org/webcasts/academiclanguage/

Schleppegrell, M. J. (2004). *The language of schooling: A functional linguistics perspective*. Mahwah, NJ: Lawrence Erlbaum Associates.

Schleppegrell, M. J., & de Oliveira, L. C. (2006). An integrated language and content approach for history teachers. *Journal of English for Academic Purposes, 5*, 254–68.

Schleppegrell, M. J., & O'Hallaron, C. L. (2011). Teaching academic language in L2 secondary settings. *Annual Review of Applied Linguistics, 31*, 3–18.

Schmidt, R. (1990). The role of consciousness in second language learning. *Applied Linguistics, 111*, 17–46.

Schmidt, R. (2001). Attention. In P. Robinson (Ed.), *Cognition and second language instruction* (pp. 3–32). Cambridge: Cambridge University Press.

Schulz, R. A. (2001). Cultural differences in student and teacher perceptions concerning the role of grammar teaching and corrective feedback: USA–Colombia. *Modern Language Journal, 85*, 244–58.

Segalowitz, N. (2010). *Cognitive bases of second language fluency*. New York: Routledge.

Serrano, R. (2011). From metalinguistic instruction to metalinguistic knowledge, and from metalinguistic knowledge to performance in error correction and oral production tasks. *Language Awareness, 20*, 1–16.

Shin, S. (2009). Negotiating grammatical choices: Academic language learning by secondary ESL students. *System, 37*, 391–402.

Short, D. J. (2002). Language learning in sheltered social studies classes. *TESOL Journal, 11*, 18–24.

Short, D. J., Echevarria, J., & Richards-Tutor, C. (2011). Research on academic literacy development in sheltered instruction classrooms. *Language Teaching Research, 15*, 363–80.

Simpson-Vlach, R. C., & Ellis, N. C. (2010). An academic formulas list: New methods in phraseology research. *Applied Linguistics, 31*, 487–512.

Slavin, R. (1994). *Cooperative learning, second edition*. Boston: Allyn and Bacon.

Slavin, R., & Cheung, A. (2005). A synthesis of research on language of reading instruction for English Language Learners. *Review of Educational Research, 75,* 247–81.

Snow, M. A. (1998). Trends and issues in content-based instruction. *Annual Review of Applied Linguistics, 18*, 243–67.

Snow, M. A., & Brinton, D. (Eds.). (1997) *The content-based classroom: Perspectives on integrating language and content.* White Plains: Addison Wesley Longman.

Snow, M. A., Met, M., & Genesee, F. (1989). A conceptual framework for the integration of language and content in second/foreign language instruction. *TESOL Quarterly, 23*, 201–17. Reprinted in P. A. Richard-Amato & M. A. Snow (Eds.). (1992), *The multicultural classroom: Readings for content-area teachers* (pp. 27–38). Reading, MA: Addison-Wesley.

Spada, N., & Lightbown, P. M. (2002). L1 and L2 in the education of Inuit children in Northern Quebec: Abilities and perceptions. *Language and Education, 16*, 212–40.

Spada, N., & Lightbown, P. M. (2008). Form-focused instruction: Isolated or integrated? *TESOL Quarterly, 42,* 181–207.

Spilka, I. (1976). Assessment of second language performance in immersion programs. *Canadian Modern Language Review, 32,* 543–61.

Stern, H. H. (1984). The immersion phenomenon. *Language and Society.* Ottawa: Ministry of Supply and Services.

Stern, H. H. (1985). The time factor and compact course development. *TESL Canada Journal. 3*, 13–27.

Swain, M. (1981a). Linguistic expectations: Core, extended and immersion programs. *The Canadian Modern Language Review 40*, 486–97.

Swain, M. (1981b). Time and timing in bilingual education. *Language Learning 31*, 1–15.

Swain, M. (1988). Manipulating and complementing content teaching to maximize second language learning. *TESL Canada Journal, 6*, 68–83.

Swain, M. (2005). The output hypothesis: Theory and research. In E. Hinkel (Ed.), *Handbook of research in second language teaching and learning* (pp. 471–83). Mahwah, NJ: Lawrence Erlbaum Associates.

Swain, M., & Carroll, S. (1987). The immersion observation study. In B. Harley, P. Allen, J. Cummins, & M. Swain (Eds.), *Development of bilingual proficiency: Final report. Vol. II: Classroom treatment* (pp. 190–316). Toronto, ON: Modern Language Centre, OISE/UT.

Swain, M., & Lapkin, S. (1982). *Evaluating bilingual education: A Canadian case study*. Clevedon, UK: Multilingual Matters.

Swain, M., & Lapkin, S. (1998). Interaction and second language learning: Two adolescent French immersion students working together. *Modern Language Journal, 82*, 320–37.

Swain, M., & Lapkin, S. (2001). Focus on form through collaborative dialogue: Exploring task effects. In M. Bygate, P. Skehan, & M. Swain (Eds.), *Researching pedagogic tasks: Second language learning, teaching and testing* (pp. 99–118). London: Longman.

Swain, M., & Lapkin, S. (2002). Talking it through: Two French immersion learners' response to reformulation. *International Journal of Educational Research 37*, 285–304.

Swain, M., & Lapkin, S. (2005). The evolving sociopolitical context of immersion education in Canada: Some implications for program development. *International Journal of Applied Linguistics, 15,* 169–86.

Tabors, P., & Snow, C. (1994). English as a second language in preschool programs. In F. Genesee (Ed.), *Educating second language children: The whole child, the whole curriculum, the whole community* (pp. 103–25). Cambridge: Cambridge University Press.

Tan, M. (2011). Mathematics and science teachers' beliefs and practices regarding the teaching of language in content learning. *Language Teaching Research, 15,* 325–42.

Tan, M., & Lan, K. H. (2011). Teaching mathematics and science in English in Malaysian classrooms: The impact of teacher beliefs on classroom practices and student learning. *Journal of English for Academic Purposes 10*, 5–18.

Tarone, E., & Swain, M. (1995). A sociolinguistic perspective on second-language use in immersion classrooms. *The Modern Language Journal, 79,* 166–78.

Tedick, D. J., Christian, D., & Fortune, T. W. (Eds.). (2011). *Immersion education: Practices, policies, possibilities.* Bristol, UK: Multilingual Matters.

Teemant, A., Bernhardt, E., Rodríguez-Muñoz, M. (1997). Collaborating with content-area teachers: What we need to share. In M. A. Snow & D. Brinton (Eds.), *The content-based classroom: Perspectives on integrating language and content* (pp. 311–18). White Plains: Addison Wesley Longman. Reprinted from 1996 *TESOL Journal 5*, 16–20.

Tembe, J., & Norton, B. (2008). Promoting local languages in Ugandan primary schools: The community as stakeholder. *The Canadian Modern Language Review, 65,* 33–60.

Thomas, W. P., & Collier, V. P. (1997). *School effectiveness for language minority children.* Washington, DC: National Clearinghouse for Bilingual Education. Retrieved September 12, 2012 (pdf) from www.thomasandcollier.com

Thomas, W. P., & Collier, V. P. (2003). *What we know about: Effective instructional approaches for language minority learners.* Arlington, VA: Educational Research Service.

Toohey, K. (2000). *Learning English at school: Identity, social relations and classroom practice.* Clevedon, UK: Multilingual Matters.

Trofimovich, P., & McDonough, K. (Eds.). (2011). *Applying priming methods to L2 learning, teaching and research: Insights from psycholinguistics.* Amsterdam: John Benjamins.

Turnbull, M., Hart, D., & Lapkin, S. (2003). Grade 6 French immersion students' performance on large-scale reading, writing, and mathematics tests: Building explanations. *The Alberta Journal of Educational Research, 49*, 6–23.

Turnbull, M., Lapkin, S., & Hart, D. (2001). Grade 3 immersion students' performance in literacy and mathematics: Province-wide results from Ontario (1998–99). *Canadian Modern Language Review, 58*, 9–26.

Turnbull, M., Lapkin, S., Hart, D., & Swain, M. (1998). Time on task and immersion graduates' French proficiency. In S. Lapkin (Ed.), *French second language education in Canada: Empirical studies* (pp. 31–55). Toronto, ON: University of Toronto Press.

Unz, R. (1997, October 19). Bilingual is a damaging myth. *Los Angeles Times*.

VanPatten, B. (1988). The acquisition of clitic pronouns in Spanish: Two case studies. *Language Learning, 38*, 243–60.

VanPatten, B. (1990). Attending to form and content in the input. *Studies in Second Language Acquisition, 12*, 287–301.

Wajnryb, R. (1990). *Grammar dictation*. Oxford: Oxford University Press.

White, J. (1998). Getting the learners' attention: A typographical input enhancement study. In C. Doughty & J. Williams (Eds.), *Focus on form in classroom second language acquisition* (pp. 85–113). Cambridge: Cambridge University Press.

White, J. (2008). Speeding up acquisition of *his* and *her*: Explicit L1/L2 contrasts help. In J. Philp, R. Oliver, & A. Mackey (Eds.), *Second language acquisition and the younger learner: Child's play?* (pp. 193–228). Amsterdam: John Benjamins.

Wong Fillmore, L. (1983). The language learner as an individual: Implications of research on individual differences for the ESL teacher. In M. A. Clarke & J. Handscombe (Eds.), *On TESOL '82: Pacific perspectives on language learning and teaching* (pp. 157–273). Washington, DC: TESOL.

Wong Fillmore, L. (2000). Loss of family languages: Should educators be concerned? *Theory into Practice, 39*, 203–10.

Wong Fillmore, L. (2010). Common core standards: Can English learners meet them? Accessed on May 2, 2012.

Wong Fillmore, L., & Snow, C. (2000). What teachers need to know about language. ERIC Clearinghouse on Languages and Linguistics. Special Report.

Wray, A. (2000). Formulaic sequences in second language teaching: principle and practice. *Applied Linguistics, 21*, 463–89.

Zimmerman, C. B. (2009). *Word knowledge: A vocabulary teacher's handbook*. Oxford: Oxford University Press.

Zwiers, J. (2006). Integrating academic language, thinking, and content: Learning scaffolds for non-native speakers in the middle grades. *Journal of English for Academic Purposes 5*, 317–32.

Index

(Page numbers annotated with 'g' and 't' refer to glossary entries or tables respectively.)